A SANDWICH FOR THE JOURNEY

THE STORY OF A LONDON EVACUEE

CHARLES C. MINX, JR.

Published by NEWTYPE Publishing
newtypepublishing.com

ISBN: 978-1-949709-91-9
eISBN: 978-1-949709-92-6

Printed in the United States.

This book is dedicated to my second father, Maurice Levitt, and to all those child evacuees whose stories remain untold.

ACKNOWLEDGMENTS

First and foremost, I would like to express my deepest gratitude to my director, Dr. Monica Tetzlaff, without whose time commitment, encouragement, patient guidance, and a shared sense of humor the completion of this book could not have been realized. Peace, Monica. I also wish to thank Dr. Lisa Zwicker for her insightful comments and suggestions for revision – bringing out the "inner-historian" in me. I am also very much indebted to Dr. Ken Smith who once introduced me to the beautiful world of book design, and helped me appreciate the beauty therein. Without Dr. Smith's guidance, I might still be transcribing the many hours of recorded interview dialogue. Keep on rockin' in the free world, Ken. My heartfelt appreciation goes to the late David James who spent so many hours of his time helping me physically transform my graduate thesis into a beautiful, attractive book, as only he could. Thank you, David. Special recognition goes out to Dr. Joseph Chaney, our MLS director, who set me on this amazing path of learning, intellectual discourse, and introspection. Thank you for believing in me, Joe. And how can I forget my wonderful wife, Laura, who sacrificed so much, including many of our early morning coffee chats as I sat hunched over my word processor? Thank you, Baby. Finally, I wish to thank my dear father-in-law, and the subject of this remarkable story, Maurice Levitt. Thanks, Dad for the great moments we shared working together, and for allowing me the honor of doling out just a little bit of "immortality" your way. God knows you deserve it.

CONTENTS

PROLOGUE

Mum and Dad said he'd be going on a lovely holiday. But did the parents of his hundreds of school mates arrange similar holidays for their own children? That question had never occurred to the boy's seven-year-old mind. Whatever the case, they would embark upon a well-ordered exodus down the local high street en route to East Hackney's Dalston railway station. First, the children were dropped off at Queensbridge Road school by their parents (who had no knowledge of their charges' destinations). Once there, they were handed over to their teachers who lined them up by class to be marched to the aforementioned rail station.

The boy sensed a tangible excitement along with a considerable dose of fear in the air as he queued up in the assembly area with the other children and their teachers. Each student had brought a parcel (or perhaps a small suitcase) containing the most basic of personal belongings. Around their necks hung both a personal identification tag and a small box ominously housing a government-issued gas mask—curious belongings, indeed for holiday goers. Having ensured all the children were present and accounted for and were properly fitted-out, their teachers led them onto the street—not unlike a group of runners about to begin a marathon race the throngs of children began their trek rather bunched-up. The initial going was slow yet steady, but at last, they were on their way. After a few blocks, their pace had quickened and the sounds of hundreds of hard leather shoes on the tarmac mixed with the melodic chatter of excited children's voices had taken on a mesmerizing, almost musical life of its own.

Before long the music gave-way to the sound of hurried, heavy footsteps accompanied by labored breathing. Suddenly, the boy felt a strong hand on his shoulder. As he turned around he discovered who its owner was. It was his father! Had he come to accompany him on this mysterious holiday? Perhaps he was here to take him home. It was neither. His father looked down on the boy with his warm, blue, rather moistened eyes as he stuffed a paper bag of unknown contents into the lad's coat pocket. A slight smile spread across the man's face as he softly said, "It's a sandwich... for your journey. You'll be hungry." With that, his father turned on his heel and nearly as quickly as he appeared—was gone. The music resumed and just like that the boy was whisked away by the surging storm of his classmates into an unknown future.

INTRODUCTION

The familiar aroma of Thanksgiving dinner emanated from my mother-in-law's kitchen as my family sat around the Levitt dining room table anticipating the annual feast. I, however, was experiencing a different sort of anticipation than the kind driven by a person's appetite. Mine was the sort that one feels when he is about to pose a long put-off question that might well change the lives of both parties involved. Before the cranberry sauce hit the table I decided to simply ask: "Dad, how would you like it if I wrote a book about your experiences as an evacuee during the war for my graduate thesis project?" My father-in-law's response was better than I could have imagined. His usually tired, somewhat haunted eighty-three-year-old eyes sparkled brightly, and, without a glance in my direction, he shouted into the kitchen, "Naomi, Charles is going to write a book about me." I had my answer.

There is an intrinsic value to be found in every human being's story whether it comes in the form of a lesson learned, an example to emulate or avoid, a validation of the course one's life has taken, or simply a good read. History and literature are full of thousands of such stories, based upon characters real and imagined. It is the duty of a historian and a writer of literature to scour history and churn up the pools of imagination in search of these stories and pass them along, extending the gift of immortality to the story's owner. I have found one such story to tell you, my reader, and I hope to ensure the legacy of its hero for years to come.

This is the story of my dear father-in-law, Maurice Levitt, who, as a young boy from East Hackney, London, found himself caught up in the horrors of the Second World War, which turned up in his own back yard or, as he put it, "my back garden." Between 1939 to 1944, at the age of seven to twelve, Maurice was evacuated five times from his family's home and forced to live with "host" families in the English and Welsh countryside.

In the first few days of September of 1939 nearly 3 million people, mostly children, were evacuated through the largest population movement in British History: "Operation Pied Piper." It may appear that Maurice's story, although interesting and heartfelt, is just one of the many that emerged from the ashes of London. So what is it about this story which merits its telling and allows it to stand out?

This story of a young boy and his father who had to part ways during the time of war has an underlying issue that asks: "At what cost did this 'safekeeping' come?" The answer to this question shall become evident within my narrative as we relive the experiences of this inner-city boy who was severed from the love, support, and traditions of his family, and placed in a rural existence—often with unreceptive households.

Another element that makes this account important is that it is the story of a *Jewish* child evacuee—the son of a Polish Immigrant. His being Jewish made gaining acceptance by both his "host" families and the gentile children he encountered a challenge at times. The most important ingredient to this aspect of Maurice's story was provided by his father, Abram, who refused to seek shelter during the nightly bombing raids—opting to ride it out alone within the rooms of his house. His is a much more somber contribution to the story, however, as we shall soon discover. Above all else, it is the preservation of Maurice's legacy that necessitates the telling of this story. When I recall that sparkle in his eyes as he learned about this book I knew something wonderful was happening—the rekindling of an old man's spirit.

I first met Maurice at his home in Santa Maria, California in the autumn of 1991 when I picked up his daughter, Laura for a date. With embarrassment, I remember my failed attempt to win over Maurice and his wife Naomi by projecting an "All American Boy" persona. Sporting a baseball cap and chomping on bubble gum, I came to collect their English bred daughter. To my horror, Laura soon confided to me that her father asked: "Just who is this Charles bloke—who you say is ten years older than you—turning up at my house chomping on chewing gum like some kind of a bloody 'hick'?" After that beginning, things had to get better. They did. We married five years later.

Over the years our family has faced more than its share of adversity. In 2002, Laura was diagnosed with multiple sclerosis. Three years later we were told our youngest daughter was on the Autism spectrum. Life challenges such as these have brought us closer together—so close, that I now consider Maurice to be my second father, while he has come to regard me as his second son.

We trust each other, and the presence of trust between the re-searcher and his subject is vital to the success of any oral history project. From the beginning, I made it clear that my primary mo-tivation for writing this book lay in the knowledge that it meant so much to him. This has allowed him to speak freely as we con-ducted our six interview sessions in the office of his South Bend, Indiana home—a familiar, comfortable setting where we were at ease. Here, I encouraged Maurice to simply relate what was on his mind as I gently guided his responses to my questions.

A family vacation in England in 2001 provided me with the opportunity to explore London (including East Hackney) and the surrounding English countryside. As we conducted our inter-views fourteen years later my memories of these places brought life to Maurice's childhood recollections. While in England, Mau-rice and I spent a day at the Royal Air Museum in Hendon. This provided me with some perspective when he recalled some of the same aircraft and "wonder weapons" deployed during the Battle of Britain.

My experience telling Maurice's story did not come without certain challenges. Consider my wife's perpetual question over the course of the project's interview phase: "So, what did Dad say, to-day?"—to which my patent response was: "Wait until the book is finished, baby." Then there was the time early on in the interview process when Maurice concluded his rendition of a delightful, yet embarrassing anecdote with: "Keep it to yourself, Charles—I don't want Laura hearing about this." Thankfully, that was the only time we encountered that particular "family-exclusive" restriction. I could be overly cautious to not offend Maurice's feelings as I posed my questions and put his story into words—certainly to a greater extent than had I been working with a stranger. This was never a major obstacle, yet it was something I periodically had to overcome over the course of the project. All things considered, I can say without hesitation, that the advantages far outweigh the disadvantages in terms of my experience working with a loved one—indeed, with the man I consider to be my second father. The fruits of that experience shall soon be revealed, but first, let us take a look back at Maurice's familial roots with an emphasis upon his extraordinary mother known as Cissy.

CHAPTER ONE

CISSY

Like most of London's Jewish population, both sides of Maurice's family immigrated from Eastern Europe—Poland, specifically. His maternal grandfather and grandmother put down roots in London during the later years of the Victorian Age, or sometime in the 1880s by best accounts. Upon his arrival in England, Issac Saunderson purchased a house and opened a kosher butcher shop in London's somewhat seedy, yet ever-vibrant East End. Shortly thereafter he wed his second wife, Leah. The butcher shop, located on the first floor of their house, with the cramped rooms on the second floor serving as the Saunderson family's domicile, allowed them to make ends meet and feed their growing family, but little more. Sadly, Issac died of a sudden heart attack in 1918 at the age of 52, leaving his widow with the daunting task of running the business *and* providing for her seven children: sons Simon, Alf (nicknamed "Pommie"), Mark and Puddie, along with daughters Anne, Hetty and Cissy, Maurice's mother, who was the firstborn on the 5th of May, 1905.

With the passing of Issac, a very hard life became even harder, especially for Cissy who, as the eldest, assumed more than her share of responsibility and was given a greater workload than her six siblings. As a young girl, she was required to spend hours after excru-ciating hours in the basement of their home, hunched over an old laun-dry tub and washboard scrubbing her family's laundry until her hands were rubbed raw. Once Sissy reached her teens she could be found in the butcher shop cutting meat (always in accordance with strict kosher law), preparing orders and waiting on cus-tomers under the scrutinizing watch of her ever-stern mother, Leah who sat stoically by in her rocking chair crocheting away.

The tombstone of Maurice's grandfather "Isaac"

An argument could easily be made that this was not much of a life for a blossoming teenage girl who was quite beautiful in her own right. Indeed, Cissy was often the target of flirtations of the neighborhood boys (and also men, including a particularly dash-ing fellow with the colorful name of "Shark Silver") who visited the shop regularly, presumably for its delicious salt-beef sandwiches, but more aptly for a chance to be waited on, and perhaps draw a smile from this charming young woman. This did not escape the eyes or ears of her mother, who only spoke Yiddish while in the butcher shop. It was becoming quite clear to Leah that Cissy was fast becoming a woman. The time had come to honor the wishes of her late husband, Isaac who put into his last will and testament the directive that their eldest daughter was to be the first to marry. Getting to work, in earnest, on an arranged marriage to a suitable young Jewish man was now in order.

As things turned out, Leah did not have to wait long before Providence came knocking in the personage of one Sarah Levitt, a regular customer of the shop. One day in 1928 she entered the shop bearing exciting news regarding the "availability" of a certain cousin of hers named Abram (Alf) Levitt, a successful tailor who, according to her, "made good money." Abram was exactly the type of hard-working successful man Leah had in mind for her daughter, so she immediately made plans for them to meet. Cissy, however, received the news with something less than enthusiasm, to say the least. In fact, she was absolutely appalled at the idea of being coerced into marrying this Polish immigrant who had been in the country for less than three years, and could barely speak a word of English! Her mother would have none of it, and promptly carried-on with arranging their marriage—the first step being Abram's purchase of the engagement ring. Little did Leah know she was playing right into the hands of Cissy's plan.

Soon after their initial meeting Abram and Cissy found themselves strolling down the local high street. Suddenly, Abram stopped in front of the display window of a jewelry store where he casually instructed Cissy to go ahead and pick-out her engagement ring. She played right into his hands when she boldly proclaimed, "Very well then, but I will only agree to marry you if you buy me the exact ring I choose." With that, she selected the ring with the largest diamond that was on display, quite assured that this tailor could not possibly afford it, thereby thwarting their engagement

before it even started. To her shock and dismay, he confidently walked into the store, pulled out his wallet and purchased the ring of her heart's desire. The little Polish immigrant had called her bluff. As things turned out the fox had out-foxed the vixen. Cissy had little choice but to agree to award him with her hand in marriage.

Abram Levitt aka "Alf"

When the wedding day arrived our young beauty's feelings toward her fiance had not changed one iota—if anything they had hardened. While she was reluctantly getting ready for the nuptials a heated argument with her mother ensued. Cissy took one last stand against Leah, looked her right in the eye and adamantly refused to marry Abram. This final act of defiance resulted in a hard slap across her face, courtesy of her mother who icily informed her daughter, in no uncertain terms, "You *will* marry this man today!" There would be no more effort to resist her fate. The wedding would go on as scheduled.

The year was 1928, and ten years had gone by since Isaac's untimely passing. Over that time Leah and the children had managed to make a go of the butcher shop. In fact, it had grown into a viable business turning-out a tidy profit. Consequently, she was able to throw an elegant, some might say extravagant wedding for her eldest daughter. Isaac would have been pleased.

The ceremony, which was held at the venerable Hackney Synagogue, could have been a scene right out of "The Great

Gatsby". Friends and family alike arrived in droves, all doing their best to "Put on the Ritz." The guests turned out in their absolute finest with the men sporting their traditional top hats (also known as  "toppers"), and the women donning stylish, snug-fitting "cloche" hats—all the rage in the 1920s. Once their vows were said, and the union was consummated with a resounding "Mazel tov!", the time had come to celebrate.

In keeping with just one of the many Jewish traditions, the wedding reception found the male guests queuing up to take a turn dancing with the bride. Abram would have none of that as he stubbornly refused to allow anyone to steal a dance with his betrothed. At surface level this might appear to have been an act of selfishness, or possibly an indication of some serious control issues on his part, however viewing this under a more optimistic light, one might conclude that his actions could serve testament to his adoration and love for Cissy, who he clearly treasured and continued to do so for the next sixty-plus years.

During the following ten years which preceded the beginning of World War II, the couple settled into the routine of married life. Shortly before the wedding, Abram had purchased a house that was located just down the street from Leah's. This was convenient for Cissy who continued to spend her days working in the butcher shop while her husband set off each morning to practice his trade as a tailor—laboring for various garment manufacturers in London—some not much more than sweat-shops. It was not an easy life for either, but they got by well  enough to consider planning a family of their own. Then, in 1930, tragedy struck the Levitt household. Cissy, who was pregnant for the first time, suffered the heartbreak of the still-born delivery of a baby girl she had carried full-term. The young couple was understandably devastated but, nevertheless, resolved to try again.

Two years later Cissy and Abram Levitt were blessed with the birth of a beautiful, healthy baby boy.

They named him Maurice after Cissy's favorite crooner Maurice Chevalier.

Little did they know the twisted turn fate held in store for their little family, for in seven short years their precious child would be numbered among the throngs of inner-city English children in Great Britain's ambitious child evacuation program code-named: "Operation Pied Piper."

CHAPTER TWO

OPERATION PIED PIPER

The Phony War

With Neville Chamberlain's failure at the Munich Confer-
ence and the subsequent German occupation of Prague and the
rest of Czechoslovakia in 1938, it had become brutally apparent
that all efforts to "appease" the enormous ego and ambitions of
Adolf Hitler through the conventional avenues of diplomacy had
been in vain. Reluctantly, the government of Great Britain began
to brace itself for the inevitability of war on its home front with
the German Third Reich, and all that implied in terms of safeguarding its civilian population—especially the children. Author
Niko Gartner describes the British government's unprecedented undertaking in his book, *Operation Pied Piper: The Wartime
Evacuation of Schoolchildren from London and Berlin 1938-46*:
"During that summer, preparations were evident all over London: houses were made ready for blackouts, sandbags were piled
outside municipal buildings, and Anderson shelters were deliv-

ered and set up."[1] With dreadful anticipation, the people of Great Britain began to wait for Hitler to make his next move.

As things turned out, they were in for a long wait. The eight-month period between the conclusion of Hitler's "lightning" Polish campaign in mid-September 1939 until the invasion of France in May 1940 found the war settling into what was essentially a waiting phase for the two world powers that was aptly coined: "The Phony War."[2] Eventually the German Blitzkrieg arrived in Western Europe as it came crashing through the Ardennes Forest into France during the late spring of 1940.

The Battle of Britain was soon to follow. Finally, for the subjects of King George VI, the wait was nearing its end.

Preparations for Evacuation

Initial preparations for a possible evacuation of a large portion of the civilian sector of Great Britain began in 1931 with the creation of the Imperial Defense Committee's "Evacuation Subcommittee"—an organization whose activities greatly accelerated in the mid-1930s in response to the rather alarming buildup of Hitler's Luftwaffe. During the summer of 1938, plans were further developed by the Anderson Committee and were subsequently implemented by the Royal Ministry of Health. This is the same Sir John Anderson to whom the completion of thousands of "back garden" bomb shelters owe their collective names. Anderson's scheme called for the Island Kingdom to be partitioned into three zones, each comprising roughly one-third of the nation's

---

1 Niko Gartner, Operation Pied Piper: The Wartime Evacuation of Schoolchildren from London and Berlin 1938-46 (Charlotte: Information Age Publishing, Inc., 2012), 56.
2 Richard J. Evans, The Third Reich at War (New York: The Penguin Press, 2009), 112.

population. Each zone was to bear the classification as either "evacuation" (large urban centers), "neutral" (areas equally positioned between a rural area and a populous urban center), or "reception" (strictly rural areas). In effect, the zone's designation was dependent upon its *likelihood* of becoming a viable target of the German bombing campaign, as the aerial bombing was the greatest perceived threat to the civilian population, at that time. Try as they might, no safeguarding measures could hope to be 100% effective as a spokesman of the British government relates in author Carlton Jackson's study of Operation Pied Piper, "In a country the size of England, there is, in the condition of modern war, no place of absolute safety."

The majority of the children who were earmarked for evacuation by the government were born between the years 1924 and 1938 putting them roughly between the ages of one and fifteen years of age. Categories of priority for evacuation were established as follows: Category "A" was comprised of school children between the ages of five and fifteen. This group was to be evacuated en masse, by school, accompanied by their teachers who had them well prepared through the constant evacuation drills they rehearsed over and over. This category accounted for some twenty percent of the children who were evacuated during the war. Category "B" was the most problematic as it consisted of children under the age of five. As such, these children had never attended school. Therefore they had never been exposed to the drills the older children experienced in preparation for the evacuation. This almost complete lack of preparedness led to disorganization that sometimes bordered upon chaos when the time came for these youngsters to be evacuated. Further, the government encouraged the children's mothers to accompany them, making things more difficult for the hosts in the reception areas. If these children were placed in their reception families unaccompanied, the head of his or her new household was given what amounted to parenting authority sanctioned by, and under the close supervision of, the local authorities. This category comprised almost eighty percent of the total. Category "C" was created for sightless children who were scheduled for second-day evacuations due to the time-consuming policy of informing their parents of their imminent evacuation in person rather than over the wireless. This was done for security reasons. Finally, Category "D" was reserved for expectant mothers. They too were scheduled for evacuation on the second day. Provisions were made for these women and their unborn children in terms of evacuation prioritization dependent upon their varying stages of pregnancy. More often than not, pregnant women evacuated to "neutral sites" to provide for their safety while allowing them proximity performed to medical centers.[3]

The government preferred that the plotting of the routes between the schools and the train stations (or other "control points" that were earmarked for embarkation) be performed by teachers and headmasters.[4] For the sake of British morale, and in an attempt to deprive Herr Goebbels (Hitler's Minister of Propaganda and Public Enlightenment) of any additional fuel for his already well-running propaganda machine, mass rehearsals of

---

3 Ibid., 17.
4 Niko Gartner, "Administering 'Operation Pied Piper'—How the London County Council Prepared for the Evacuation of its Schoolchildren 1938-1939." Journal of Educational Administration & History 42, no. 1 (February 2010): 26.

thousands of children were avoided, at all costs. This was part of the government's policy of practicing what came to be termed "rehearsing without rehearsals." Police cars laden with loudspeakers were deployed, pamphlets were distributed, and posters were put up to spread the message throughout the urban neighborhoods to parents alerting them to the impending need to evacuate their children.

The message was also quite effectively conveyed via speakers who frequented public gatherings delivering a government-approved "set speech" that encouraged thousands of parents to sign up their charges.

Suppose war was to come…what would you do with your children? We have to assume that bombers would come over and certainly they would carry and drop a far greater load of bombs than in the last war. Moreover, big and crowded cities offer tremendous temptation to a ruthless enemy. Would you not prefer to entrust your children to their teachers, to take them to some safer place?[5]

By war's end, this massive undertaking eventually saw the evacuation of nearly four million people (mostly children) to the

---

5 Jackson, Who will Save our Children?, 18., quoted in Housing and Local Government report, February and September 1939.

relative safety of the English countryside and to a lesser degree, to the nations of the British Commonwealth and the United States, making it the largest and most concentrated mass movement of humanity in British history.[6]

The First Wave: September 1939—January 1940

One fact that has been somewhat lost to history is that the first significant evacuation actually occurred in 1938—well before Great Britain's declaration of war. This mass movement of humanity saw the evacuation of over 4,000 physically handicapped London children to the safety of the English countryside. This, however, proved to be a drop in the bucket when compared to what was soon to come. The ambitious evacuation program that followed was, somewhat ironically, code-named Operation Pied Piper after the rather disturbing German folktale of the same title.

Evacuations of Britain's large urban centers began in earnest with the activation of the governments "Clean-Out scheme,"[7] when Hitler's armed forces, without provocation, boldly invaded Poland on September 1st, 1939. Two days later, Great Britain formally declared war against Nazi Germany World War II had begun.

On this fateful first day of wartime evacuations, parents were notified by local war information messages (LOWENS) to send

---

6 Ibid., 147.
7 Ibid., 26.

their children to school as normal, bearing suitcases and or knapsacks packed with whatever they deemed necessary for the journey to the reception areas. Open arriving at school they were, as rehearsed, formed into squads of fifty students and marched by their teachers to the nearest railway station for evacuation to the reception zones. Secrecy was paramount to the British government, therefore most children (and their parents) had no idea where they were, or where they were going. Many children were told they were going on a great adventure—a holiday. Some were even given pails and shovels by their parents, after having been told they were off to the seashore. German spies were also a concern, so workers were hired with instructions to tear down all the signs bearing the names of the railway stations in route to the reception areas. Some of this was done on the day the trains were passing through.

When one considers the plethora of challenges inherent with an evacuation of this scope, one has to conclude that this initial wave of Operation Pied Piper was nothing short of astounding success. 1,473,391 evacuees had made it safely to the reception areas, without incident, in a span of just four days. Less than one week later an additional 2 million were successfully evacuated from Britain's major cities.[8]

The children eventually arrived at their designated destinations in a tired, nervous, sometimes filthy, and more often than not, frightened state. If they were not directly received by their prearranged "hosts" (which was usually the best scenario for them), they were unceremoniously "herded" into large reception

8 Ibid., 29.

areas—often a village hall or similar. In one particularly disturbing case, the children were actually congregated, en masse, into a Lincolnshire cattle market![9]

The overall experience of being selected by the host in the various reception areas could often become a source of great psychological trauma, especially in terms of damaging the children's self-esteem. "It was to these places that the hosts came and picked whomever they wanted to keep. Little wonder, then, that forever afterward, the 'vacs' referred to these distribution points as slave markets."[10] For these frightened, exhausted children the ordeal of being passed over by a prospective host family was far more traumatic than, for instance, experiencing the indignity of being the last child picked for a team in grammar school gym class—which was about as close as most American children of the time would have come to experiencing similar feelings of rejection.

One extreme example which illustrates the hosts' reluctance to unconditionally accept their new guests, albeit on a much grander scale, occurred eleven short days after the evacuations began. Five busloads of children from the east end of London were sent back to the capital because their prospective host families simply wanted nothing to do with what they termed: "slum dwellers." The lot was often worse for Czech, Polish or even German refugee children who were evacuated alongside their English counterparts. To their unreceptive hosts these ragged "foreign foreigners", as they referred to them, received the brunt of the villagers disdain toward all evacuees in general.[11]

---

9 Ibid.
10 Ibid.
11 Jackson, Who will Take Our Children?, 31.

In all fairness, it should be pointed out that most hosts enthusiastically took their young evacuees (and in some cases their mothers) into their homes typically welcoming them with a cup of tea, a hot meal, and a soft, warm bed in which to get some much-needed sleep. For many, this was the beginning of a life long relationship between the host family and the children they took into their homes. Some evacuees even chose to stay permanently (with the blessing of their parents and obviously their hosts) in their wonderful new homes, while others chose to relocate to the villages they had so fondly remembered—after the war.

Yet there were numerous problems to be overcome. Most, but certainly not all, evacuees came from low-income families and arrived in the reception areas in a filthy, often verminous, lice-infested state. They came from a world of squalor, for lack of a better word, and consequently, did not always know what to think about, or how to receive some of the comparatively modern amenities and hygienic practices that were prevalent in their new homes. One woman, who was charged with the care of one such child, expressed her frustration and dismay over this issue in a letter to a friend: "What can be done with a child who takes a newspaper and goes into a corner of the dining room instead of using the lavatory?"[12]

Jackson also writes that some children had refused to eat their meals unless they were sitting on the floor as was the custom in their London homes. Then, there was the heart-wrenching story of a young boy who refused to sleep lying down but rather in-

---

12 Ibid., 32.

sisted upon sleeping sitting up against his bedpost as he was his nightly custom in his overcrowded East End flat.[13]

There was, however, a silver lining in all this. The evacuations shed a much-needed light upon the abhorrent conditions in which the urban working-class population was forced to live. As a consequence of these "revelations," the British government initiated long-overdue post-war reforms in the areas of national health care, housing, and nutrition, setting the stage for the comprehensive social welfare programs, which exist to this day. On some levels, the claim can be made that the evacuation of 1939 served as the impetus for the long-awaited transition of the old Britain into a newer, dare I say, better Britain.[14] Clearly, something good had come out of something quite bad, indeed.

Shortly after the Christmas of 1939 had come and gone the children began to return to their homes in the urban centers all across Britain. Nearly one-half of the original evacuees had returned home by early 1940. Realizing, perhaps foolishly, that a German attack from the air might not be imminent after all, the subjects of King George VI's island realm settled into a period of uneasy anticipation as they collectively awaited Hitler's next move. The "Phony War" was now in full force.[15]

The Second Wave: June 1940—December 1941

John Welshman sets an ominous tone for the prospect of war on the British home front in his book, Churchill's Children: "In the

---

13 Ibid.
14 Ibid., 35.
15 Gartner, Operation Pied Piper, 64.

spring of 1940 German air attacks, from April onwards, anticipated the Battle of Britain, which would carry on into the summer and autumn."[16]

With these attacks upon the sovereign soil of the British Crown, the "Phony War" had finally come to its end.[17] It was not as if the writing was not already on the wall for England, as these air attacks were precipitated by the German occupation of the Scandinavian states of Denmark and Norway in the second week of April—the latter of which occurring despite a somewhat feeble intervention of the part of British forces which proved to be much too little and far too late to make any difference. Then, more alarmingly for the British, came the fall of the Netherlands, portions of Belgium, and Northern France to the Nazi juggernaut, in early May. With the occupation of Northern France, the German high command ordered the installation of gun emplacements positioned directly across the channel from the coast of England. And to make matters worse, British intelligence reported the stockpiling of aviation fuel in the region. It had become quite clear that the invasion of Great Britain was next on Der Fuehrer's agenda.

With the war finally coming to England via German bombing raids, and the seemingly unstoppable string of victories by the German Blitzkrieg posing a real threat of a landed invasion, the British Government once again geared up to evacuate its children from its urban population centers and its coastal towns in southern and eastern England that lay across the channel from

---

16 John Welshman, Churchill's Children (New York: Oxford University Press, Inc., 2010), 133.
17 Gartner, Operation Pied Piper, 91.

German-controlled areas in France, most notably the large port city of South Hampton. Unlike the evacuations of the "twilight war" in late 1939, this round was conducted with a much greater sense of urgency due to the aforementioned threat of German invasion.[18] For the most part, children between the ages of five to fifteen were evacuated—excluding most adults.

As the first order of business, the British government contacted the parents of children who had already been evacuated and strongly encouraged them to resist the urge to bring them home, under any circumstances, for safety's sake. Apparently, many parents had insisted that their children be returned home due to their dissatisfaction over what they termed: "poor education arrangements." Once again, the government distributed a film for the eyes and ears of parents living in the large population centers, urging them to evacuate their children or leave them in the reception areas if they currently reside there. For the most part, the government's efforts had little effect, even when the threat of making evacuation a compulsory policy was made and thousands of children remained—seeking shelter from the nightly raids in the "tubes."[19] Indeed, the general public's reaction was a combination of outright defiance, complete indifference, or unawareness, as evidenced by the fact that over half of London's school-age children still remained in the capital, with over 250,000 Londoners failing to as much as responding to their government's frantic appeal to evacuate. "...thousands of children were roaming the streets of London and

---

18 Ibid.
19 Stephen Hussey, "The School Air Raid Shelter: Rethinking Wartime Pedagogies." History of Education Quarterly 43, no. 4 (Winter 2003): 532.

other big cities, obviously delighted that they did not have to go to school."[20]

However, despite the relative ineffectiveness of the government's appeal to the parents to get their children out, Operation Pied Piper's scheduled evacuations did manage to carry on as this sec-

The Aldwych Tube Station

ond wave of evacuation got underway in late May 1940. Close to 100,000 children were evacuated in the third week of June, alone. (Many of these children were on their second go around.) By July, the number had increased to over 200,000. When the Battle of Britain (otherwise known as "the Blitz") began on 7 September 1940, children who had returned home or had remained in the cities for other reasons were evacuated. To complicate matters further, over 30,000 refugees have also arrived from continental European Continent along with 25,000 more from the Channel Islands—all requiring evacuation to the safety of Britain's reception zones. Once again the villagers and farmers in the reception areas answered the call splendidly.[21]

By no stretch of the imagination did all the support for the children in need of evacuation come from British sources. Concerned people from all over the globe responded brilliantly to the

---

20 Jackson, Who will Take Our Children?, 37.
21 Ibid., 56.

imminent threat of landed invasion of the Island Kingdom.[22] Indeed, it was during this second wave of evacuation in particular that the citizens of Great Britain's Commonwealth dominions (as well as the United States) truly rose up to collectively answer the call of their "Mother Country," as they agreed to take their English cousins into the safety of their homes across the sea. "Offers to help Britain in her hour of need came from all over the world. Individuals and governments alike responded to one Englishman's opinion that Canada and the United States were morally obligated to take Britain's children, for 'After all, this is their mother country.'"[23]

An organization known as the Committee on Overseas Children's Reception Board (COARB) was formed to facilitate these requests for overseas evacuations. This was accomplished despite the protestations of Prime Minister Winston Churchill, who was of the opinion that, first and foremost, Britain's resources must be expended upon the war effort—upon defeating the Axis powers. For this reason, overseas evacuations were mainly funded and facilitated by the private sector. "Ole Winnie's" opposition toward mass emigration of British children notwithstanding, thousands of parents were more than willing to temporarily part from their children in order to ensure their safety—even if it meant ushering them off to foreign lands across thousands of miles of "Wolf Pack" infested waters. For some parents of limited financial resources (and most of them were), the prospect of an overseas evacuation presented a unique opportunity for their children to see the

---

22 Keith A. Parker, "British evacuees in America during World War II." Journal of American Culture 17, no. 4 (Winter 94 1994)
23 Jackson, Who will Take Our Children?, 63.

world—something they never could have otherwise dreamed of. Others were off to stay with relatives who they had never met or barely remembered. For most, however, there was no motivation at play other than that of safeguarding their precious children. The fear and anxiety wrought from the prospect of bombing attacks and foreign invasion were more than enough to persuade parents to send their children thousands of miles away from home. [24]

Early in the summer of 1940, at one of the darkest moments in the history of Great Britain, over 3,000 British children were undergoing processing for evacuation to the dominions to escape the relentless bombings that seemed to be the precursor of a German invasion. This number represented a small percentage of the children in Britain at the time, and the hope was to send abroad many more thousands of children. Then disaster struck. On 17 September 1940 at 10 PM, the *City of Benares,* bound for Canada from Liverpool, was torpedoed some 600 miles  out of port. 260 passengers perished. Eighty-four were children. An immediate outcry reverberated from the chambers of allied powers proclaiming that though it is grown-up people who cause wars, it is the children who suffer.[25]

This heart-wrenching disaster spelled doom for the already controversial overseas evacuation program in Britain. All over the nation people cried out for a cessation of all international

24 Ibid., 162.
25 Ibid., 94.

evacuations. Eventually, Churchill and his Admiralty had their way, and despite the efforts of CORB, there were no further overseas evacuations after early October—much to the disappointment of the 200,000 children registered for outward transportation.[26]

Before he could hope to launch his much anticipated landed invasion of Britain, codenamed: "Operation Sea Lion," Adolf Hitler knew that he must first control the English Channel, which was presently patrolled by the Royal Navy—the most powerful naval force in the world at that time. Never a great sea power, Germany's best hope of neutralizing the Royal Navy, and thereby clearing the way across the channel for its invasion flotilla, was with its mighty Luftwaffe. Hitler and his flamboyant Reich Mar-

shall, Hermann Goering were determined to knock out the RAF by attacking its airbases—primarily in the south of England. Once they controlled the skies, they reasoned, they would be able to annihilate Britain's navy, effectively rendering the English Channel to the status of a "German Lake."

During a weather-induced lull in hostilities in mid-August, 1940 Goering declared that Germany had reached the decisive period of the air war against England with its vital task being to defeat the RAF, first and foremost it's fighter arm. And indeed, it appeared that for a change the Reich Marshall was right. From

---

26 Ibid., 98.

August 24 to September 6 the Luftwaffe sent over an average of
1,000 fighters per day, extensively damaging five forward fighter fields in southern England while severely bombing six of the
seven key sector stations to such a degree that the entire com-
munication system seemed on the verge of being knocked out.
Worse still, 466 British fighters were damaged or destroyed, and
103 RAF pilots were killed with another 128 seriously wounded,
representing one-quarter of their trained pilots. Winston Churchill later inferred in his writing that the scales had clearly tilted against fighter command. Just a few more weeks of this and
Britain would have most likely lost the ability to defend its skies,
making possible a successful German invasion of the homeland.[27]
Then, on the night of August 23, one of history's twists of fate
occurred that drastically turned the tide of the Battle of Britain
in England's favor. A minor navigational error on the part of the
pilots of twelve German bombers caused them to drop their pay-
loads not on their designated industrial targets on the outskirts
of the British capital, but rather on central London, blowing up
a number of homes and injuring some civilians. Thinking the act
deliberate, Churchill reacted immediately by ordering the RAF
to conduct its first bombing raid on Berlin proper the following
evening. A dense cloud cover over the Reich's capital rendered the
damage negligible.

However, the effect on German morale was immeasurable.
The RAF returned in greater numbers the following night, killing Berliners for the first time in the war.[28] Predictably, the Nazi

---

27 William L. Shrirer, The Rise and Fall of the Third Reich (New York: Simon and Schuster,
1960), 777.
28 Ibid.

leadership, particularly Adolf Hitler, was furious. After the third raid two nights later all of Dr. Goebbels's newspaper headlines read, "British Air Pirates over Berlin." On the afternoon of September 7[th,] the Luftwaffe's retaliation over London began in earnest with a raid consisting of 625 bombers and 648 fighters. The assault went on night after night as the German high command shifted their air strategy from an emphasis upon military targets to one which unleashed terror upon the civilian populations of Britain.[29]

This much-needed lull in hostilities allowed the RAF the opportunity to replenish its forces and repair its vital airfields. The RAF was saved. The nightly raids during the blitz took such a tremendous toll upon the Luftwaffe that by December 1940 Hitler decided to scale back his raids over Britain's cities, and canceled his plans to execute Operation Sea Lion. With the invasion of England "on the back burner," as it were, Hitler turned his predatory eyes eastward—to the Soviet Union—and prepared to launch his more ambitious campaign code named: "Operation Barbarossa." With that, the second wave of Operation Pied Piper came to an end.[30]

For the RAF, this was truly their finest hour. Britain had been saved from what would have been a ruthless, bloody, landed invasion by the heretofore undefeated German Wehrmacht. Yet, victory came at a tremendous cost in property and humanity. The British capital and other industrial cities took a terrible pounding for 57 consecutive nights from September 7 to November 3 from

---

29 Ibid., 778.
30 Evans, The Third Reich at War, 144.

an average of 200 Luftwaffe bombers daily. Despite this, British resolve never wavered, nor did its industrial production fall-off.[31]

The largest raids actually occurred six days before Christmas of 1940, killing almost 3,000 civilians. Although for all practical purposes the Battle of Britain had be-

gun to peter out in late October 1940, this did not completely mark the end of the Blitz. Nighttime bombing raids over London, Coventry, and other cities continued on a lesser scale for several more months until the campaign finally came to an end on May 1941 with some 40,000 people reported killed. Sadly, many of the killed and wounded were children whose parents did not heed the warnings of their government and participate in Operation Pied Piper.

The Third Wave: June 1944—March 1945

Token German air raids over Britain continued over the next two years—serving more like a deadly nuisance to the urban populations than as a viable means to break British resolve to continue the war. What these sporadic raids did do was prevent the children from coming home from the safety zones until late 1943, when the general consensus both at home and abroad was that it was safe to return to the large urban centers of Britain. Paying no heed to government warnings of impending "buzz bomb" attacks,

---

31 Shrirer, The Rise and Fall of the Third Reich,781.

thousands of domestic evacuees did return home at the end of 1943 and the beginning of 1944.[32] Then on June 6, 1944, only a few hours after the D Day landings, the German High Command gave orders for an immediate assault on Britain. Six days later, the Germans struck again as the first of Hitler's new "Vengeance Weapons" made its appearance. This was the V-1 or the Vergeltungswaffe 1, better known to Londoners and those in southeast England as the flying bomb or "doodlebug."[33] Coming at a time when most were convinced that the war was virtually won, this self-propelled, jet-powered "wonder weapon" had a devastating effect on morale. And, with good reason, for during the summer of 1944, nearly 5,500 civilians were killed in London and southeast England. The government's response in terms of getting the chil-

dren out of harm's way was immediate. With the advent of the buzz bomb on June 12, 1944, and its reconstituted threat against English cities and countryside, the third and final wave of evacuation got underway.[34] Citizens were urged by the government to avoid travel toward London and in the southeastern counties for fear of buzz bomb attacks.

Then on July 5th the first children accompanied by their mothers once again departed the capital. By September, over 1,000,000

---

32 Jackson, Who will Save our Children?, 119.
33 Bob Ogley, Doodlebugs and Rockets: The Battle of the Flying Bombs (Kent: Froglets Publications, 1992), 5.
34 Jackson, Who will Save our Children?, 125.

women, children, elderly, and disabled people had been evacuated in what proved to be a significant exodus from London.

The Nazi launch bases were located in northern France and Holland due to the limited range of the V-1's. Consequently, this time around the attacks were concentrated in the southeast region of England, which of course, again included the city of London. This change in the geography of relative danger and safety rendered the original categories of "Evacuation," "Neutral," and "Reception" areas quite obsolete. For example, a village in the southeast of England that was deemed a reception zone in 1939, might now be classified as an evacuation zone due to the flying bomb attacks in its region. London remained an evacuation zone as always.[35]

To its credit, the Royal Ministry of Defense also responded to this new German offensive in a timely, effective fashion. The defenses in England were strengthened immediately, as anti-aircraft guns and barrage balloons, were massed on the approaches to London. Additionally, fighter aircraft were deployed to patrol an outer defensive screen. These two decisive measures resulted in the destruction of many V-1s—gradually allowing the British defense forces to gain the upper hand until the threat diminished.[36] Yet, the Nazi Fuhrer had another deadly revenge weapon in his bag of tricks—a weapon he was eager to unleash upon the innocent citizenry of Great Britain—a weapon that was about to change the world forever. For "to the enemy armoury of manned

---

35 Ibid.
36 Ogley, Doodlebugs and Rockets, 5.

bomber and pilotless aircraft had been added a new and even more formidable weapon, the long-range rocket."[37]

This new wonder weapon was called the V-2. It traveled at over 3,600 miles per hour as it crashed to earth, without warn-

ing, via the stratosphere. Garnished with four stabilizing fins, the rocket measured 46 feet in length. The V-2 carried a deadly one-ton warhead. It took just 5 minutes from its launch in Peenemunde (a small German fishing village on the Baltic Sea about 110 miles north of Berlin) to reach its impact in southeastern England. Alarmingly, the V-2 flew far too fast and high to be tracked—let alone intercept-

ed. The effect of Hitler's latest vengeance weapon upon the nation was devastating. 1,115 V-2 rockets were launched toward Britain between September 1944 and March 1945 killing 2,612 in the city of London and 212 civilians outside the capital.[38]

Thankfully, for the future of humanity, the V-2 attacks were launched far too late in the war to affect its outcome.[39] By this time Hitler's Reich was being "pinched" on two sides—by the American, British and Free French (whose overwhelming

---

37 Norman Longmate, Hitler's Rockets: The Story of the V-2s (London: Pen & Sword Books, 2009), 15.
38 Ogley, Doodlebugs and Rockets, 5.
39 Evans, The Third Reich at War, 673.

forces had proved to be too much for the depleted Wehrmacht since the D-Day invasion) from the west, and by the Soviet Union's Red Army (which had been virtually unstoppable since their tide-turning victory at Stalingrad) from the east. For the people of London, the war ended on 27 March 1945, with the last major V-2 attack on Stepney.[40] A few days later American units captured the V-2 bases in Peenemunde, abruptly awakening Hitler from his delusional dreams of winning the war with his wonder weapons. With that, the flames of the last threat to the civilian population of Great Britain were extinguished after nearly 5 ½ years of terror from above. At long last, Britain's children, including a young Jewish boy from East Hackney, could come home—this time for good.

---

40 Gartner, Operation Pied Piper, 134.

CHAPTER THREE

THE ADVENT OF WAR

Hackney

When I think of the East End of London where the borough of Hackney is situated, my mind invariably conjures-up images of Charles Dickens' Oliver Twist and the Artful Dodger, or perhaps the clerk Bob Cratchit and his "lame", yet wise before his time son, Tiny Tim, or even of George Bernhard Shaw's Professor Henry Higgins and his beautiful, yet incorrigible protégée, Eliza Doolittle. Countless time-honored works of literature, stage, and cinematography alike have chosen this somewhat earthy, yet always charming "world within a world" as the setting for their tales of redemption, reconciliation, and most notably, courage and dogged perseverance. These are stories that bring out the best in humankind. I strongly feel that on many levels the people of London (Hackney included) carried-on and somehow managed to exemplify this "salt of the earth" persona of the

"East-Ender," as they doggedly endured the "hell from the sky" which was relentlessly unleashed upon their neighborhoods during the blitz.

The southern and eastern parts of the London Borough of Hackney were traditionally, but unofficially, regarded as being  part of East London, while the northern and western areas were considered to be part of North London. Its name may have been derived from The Old English 'Haca' meaning a hook, and in this context, the hook (or Haca) may be referring to the borough being situated on the hook-like end of the River Lea. Hackney covered an area of 7.4 square miles and its most notable geographic feature was the aforementioned River Lea.

This pre-war Hackney—though far from perfect—belonged to a simpler, entirely different world than the borough that existed during the blitz, or certainly than the Hackney of today as the author Alan Wilson vividly describes in his 2004 memoir, *Hackney Memories*:

> *The air is cleaner now. Then, the skies were always murky and the days of my Hackney childhood were lived under a perpetual hazy canopy the colour of lentil soup. After a seaside holiday, I wept when returning to Hackney and saw the dusty hues of its skies and its dull grey streets. I yearned for the*

bright colours of the seaside with its golden sands and deep blue sea. The social scene of Hackney has changed. Before the war, it was a warm place housing a mixed community: rich man, poor man, Jew and gentile all co-existed humanely in two or three-storey houses. Life then is not packaged in hygienic cellophane.[41]

Because of its dockland areas on the River Thames which stored vital goods for the war effort, the East End of London (including Hackney) became a prime target for bombing raids. Were the Luftwaffe to disable the East End, it would sever a vital part of London's supply chain, thereby weakening Great Britain as a whole. This was of such importance to the Luftwaffe's overall strategy that by 1940 the East End was known as "Target Area A" by German bombers—consequently making life extremely difficult and perilous for locals during the Blitz.

As it happened, Maurice's neighborhood, although located several miles from the dockland area, had the great misfortune of featuring another of the Luftwaffe's regular nightly targets. Not only was this target *in* his neighborhood, but it actually served as the north-south and east-west boundaries of his family's property on Graham Road. For literally, right in Maurice's back yard, there was a railroad junction complete with two iron rail bridges that crisscrossed two vitally strategic rail lines that the Luftwaffe was determined to knock-out.

---

41 Alan Wilson, Hackney Memories (Oxford: ISIS Publishing, Ltd, 2004), 18.

With the coming of war with Germany Maurice's Hackney, and indeed his young life was about to change forever, and given that his home was sitting virtually on top of a high priority German bomb site, his parents' best option in the late summer of 1939 was to sign-up their only child up for the initial wave of evacuation. With that, my telling of Maurice's story finally begins.

Maurice with his father Abram

The First Day

I arrived at the home of my wife's parents, Maurice and Naomi Levitt on the South Side of South Bend, Indiana at one-thirty in the afternoon. It was a cold grey day in early

January 2016—the kind of day that made you yearn for the return of spring, knowing fully well that you were in for a long wait. My mother-in-law, Naomi met me at the door and immediately ushered me into the house, guiding me in the direction of Maurice's office where he awaited me, "quite keen" to get started. It seemed as if nearly every time I spoke with Naomi since that fateful Thanksgiving dinner she would inquire as to when I was going to start Dad's interviews. It was almost as if she were more interested than he was, but in her defense over the course of the last several years she has essentially assumed the role of "household scheduler."

I was warmly greeted as I entered his always tidy office and offered a chair across from him. Maurice was seated behind his rather large desk in all his glory, surrounded by photographs of family members, books, technical manuals, his personal computer and stereo, and on his filing cabinet he displayed a perfectly crafted model of an RAF Spitfire fighter plane he had built and hand-painted years ago. Maurice's office, adorned with his technical manuals, computer components, and filing system was a reflection upon his life-long occupation as an engineer— this, I feel merits telling before we return to my account of our first interview.

Maurice's career path began to take shape in the spring of 1945. With the war winding down he returned to his home in East Hackney and enrolled in school. One year later his acceptance to Northampton Polytechnic in North London marked the beginning of his technical education at the age of fourteen. His curriculum included mathematics, physics, chemistry, technical drawing, and workshop training. Three years later, Maurice received his completion certificate, enabling him to enter the working world at age seventeen. Soon, he secured a position with General Electric Company (GEC) as an indentured student apprentice. With GEC, Maurice gained valuable experience working in many departments (including the firm's research laboratory which was under contract with the Ministry of Defense) while earning twenty-eight shillings per week. His arrangement with GEC also allowed him to continue his educa-

tion with Northampton Polytechnic where he completed a five-year study course earning the Higher National Certificate. Having received a deferment while working as an apprentice with GEC, Maurice began his compulsory military service with the Royal Air Force in 1956 at the advanced age of twenty-four. Again, he gained valuable training and experience to draw upon later in life, working on aircraft defense systems and maintaining construction equipment. Having completed his two-year hitch in the RAF, Maurice returned to GEC where he worked as a design draftsman from 1958-1960. Always one to draw upon his experiences, Maurice joined the ranks of the self-contracted draftsmen in 1961, working for numerous companies and taking on a vast range of projects (many military-related) for the next thirteen years.

Early in 1965, Maurice met his wife of fifty-four years, the woman who he refers to as the "Idol of my Life"—Naomi Rosefield. Six and one-half weeks later they were engaged—they married five months after that.

Their late son, David, was born in May 1966 followed by my wife Laura in January 1968.

In 1974 Maurice moved on from his career as an in-

Mr. and Mrs. Maurice Levitt

dependent contractor, accepting a position working in the engineering group of the business systems division of ITT Corporation. This proved to be a pivotal point of both his professional career and his family's life. Soon after his hire, ITT bought out Courier Systems, and Maurice was sent on a three-month business trip to Phoenix, Arizona as a member of a negotiating team. His main role was to manage the modification of Courier's products to meet the regulatory requirements for European sales. This experience not only introduced him to the growing field of product compliance but also got Maurice and Naomi contemplating a permanent move to America. Eventually, Maurice returned to England and resumed his career, but America remained indelibly on his mind. He and Naomi applied for and received their United States immigration visas in 1976, and all family members received their green cards in 1979.

Seven years after his fateful business trip, Maurice and his family immigrated to the United States and his familiar city of Phoenix. Naomi immediately went to work as a legal secretary, but it was difficult for Maurice to find work as he was

Maurice and Naomi revisit his East-Hackney home in 1980

repeatedly told he was overqualified. Three months passed until he was hired by GenRad Inc. for the position of Senior Mechanical Engineer. From 1984-1989 Maurice developed products for Marconi Instruments, a company he previously worked for in England. When the firm closed in 1989 he was once again unemployed, this time for four months.

Drawing upon his previous experience with regulatory compliance, Maurice secured a position with Network Equipment Technologies which required relocation to beautiful Santa Barbara, California, the city where Laura and I met two years later. In 1993 N.E.T. closed their Santa Barbara division resulting in yet another move, this time to N.E.T.'s corporate office in Silicon Valley. (Laura did not accompany her parents this time as she remained in Santa Barbara with yours truly). Then, in 1994 Maurice made his final career move to Larscom Inc., a Swedish telecom company in Santa Clara where he held the position of Homologation Manager. Maurice told me once that these were the happiest days of his professional life, as he was allowed to travel extensively to locations such as England, Russia, The Netherlands, Australia, Mexico, Brazil, and Argentina, often taking Naomi "along for the ride."

Shortly after 9/11, the stock market plummeted and the "Golden Age of Telecom" came to an end—resulting in the closure of numerous "dot-coms," along with wide-spread lay-offs. In 2003, Maurice joined the ranks of the unemployed as he too was laid-off. He decided retirement was in order thereby putting an end to his fifty-seven-year career in the field of engineering.

Now, back to the first day of interviewing...

'This is perfect,' I thought to myself, a comfortable and familiar setting for both of us to conduct this important oral history. Straight away, I emphasized that this was his story, and he should feel at ease to speak his mind, yet have the freedom to talk about only those things he was comfortable with discussing. I urged him to relax and enjoy himself, as I was certainly planning to have fun with this project. I also told him once again, that it was a great honor and a privilege to have the opportunity to play a role in the telling of his important story. The time had come. I reached over and set my digital voice recorder on Maurice's desk and pressed the record button. With that, I fired-away with my first question and *A Sandwich for the Journey* was underway.

What was it about your neighborhood that made it a "high-risk zone" and a target for the Luftwaffe?

Being in the center of London. The main area of targets was, first of all, the dock areas. As you know, flowing through London is the River Thames. A lot of shipping and a lot of items were housed in docks, buildings along the Thames. And therefore whenever the plane would make an attack, it sometimes missed its target, or it saw a bridge or a railway, it would try to destroy a railway, to stop any traffic moving in any direction. And in actual fact, my parents' house was on the junction of two bridges. So there were two railway lines going in, one was going east of London, and the other was going north and south.

In 2006, Maurice wrote his short yet highly detailed personal memoirs entitled: "The Memories of Maurice Levitt." Within its pages he describes the two railway lines referred to above:

Passenger trains that ran on the embankment along one side of the house and over the bridge on Graham Road were the "London North Eastern Region (LNER) Line." Passenger and goods trains that ran on the railway at the bottom of the garden were the 'London Midland and Scottish (LMS) Line." I can remember lots of troop trains running on the LMS Line in the war years, with soldiers waving to us out the windows.[42]

We shall revisit those troop trains in due course.

***

Having now "gotten our feet wet", so to speak, with Maurice's brief description of the inherent perils living in his neighborhood during the blitz, we moved on to his recollections of the events leading up to his first day as an evacuee. One thing I noticed was the grave, almost bitter tone in his voice as he told me that his first knowledge of the evacuation program had come from his parents who, quite deceitfully, informed him that he would soon be going on holiday with his classmates.

---

42 Maurice Levitt, "Memories of Maurice Levitt." (Unpublished personal memoirs, South Bend, Indiana, 2005), 4.

Do you recall the first time that you heard that they were planning to evacuate the children populations? Who told you about it?

My parents told me. That I would be going away with other children in my class. And other classes as well. Because I was only seven at the time, and therefore you had the older children who were also being sent away. Remember, in London at that time you left school at fourteen. That was the end of your education. And therefore children were being sent away, I think possibly in the ages of twelve, thirteen as well. It surprised me that I was being sent away. My parents said I was going away on holiday. And you didn't think much more of it, because, at that age, your parents tell you you're being sent away because there's going to be a war, what more would you know? You wouldn't know what a war was at the age of seven.

The following passage from his memoirs illustrates the contrast between the inability of a seven-year-old to understand the meaning of war, and the deep concern his parents felt for their future:

At the outbreak of the 1939 war, I was seven years old and did not understand the meaning of war. I remember my parents at times listening to the German radio stations

The traitor "Lord Haw-Haw"

to the shouting and high pitched voice of Hitler's speeches that of course were in German and of "Lord Haw Haw's"* speeches that were in English. After listening to these speeches, my parents always had long faces as to what was in the future.[43]

One can only imagine the thoughts going through the minds of his parents who were fluent in Yiddish (a language closely related to German) as they listened to Hitler's rants about the "evils" of international Jewry and his plans to eradicate the Jews from Europe.

Maurice continues...

You had practiced air raids mornings, which frightened you a bit, because they had the air raid sirens being positioned in different parts of the area, and when they went off, boy did you hear them. And then the "all clear" would sound the same.

How much time passed between the moment you were first forewarned that you were going on holiday, and you actually leaving the city?

Several weeks. And the whole process was that the local council informed my parents that I had to be ready on a certain day and time to be delivered to the school and what to take, and what I should be taking with me. And on that day, my parents took me to the school in the morning. And you had a little case where you had certain clothes, like pajamas, shirts, sweaters, trousers, and a label which was tied around your neck, a label with your name and address. And on that particular day, my parents took me to the school and they were all lined up and we walked from the school to the local railway station. I reckon there must

43 Levitt. "Memories of Maurice Levitt", 7
* Coined "Lord Haw-Haw" by London Daily Express radio critic Jonah Barrington, he was actually William Joyce, a British Fascist whose propaganda broadcasts from Germany were commonly heard in British homes during the war.

have been…under 200. And we're walking in lines along the pavement to the station. And there's one thing that I will never forget as long as I live. I was walking in that column from the school to the station. And my father…see they never told your parents where you were going. It was all hush-hush. And I'll always remember, I'll never forget it, that walking along the pavement, my father caught up, ran after me, and caught up with me in the line, and he had a bag, a paper bag, and he stuffed it in my coat pocket as I was walking and said, "There's a sandwich there. You'll be hungry." I'll never forget that. He stuffed it in my pocket as I was walking. As I was walking. And said, "You'll need it, you'll be hungry." I'll NEVER forget that!

Subsequent conversations with Maurice and my wife, Laura who became quite close to her grandfather over the years, revealed Abram to be a man of few open displays of affection. That simple act of kindness by his father as he "stuffed" a sandwich in his son's pocket may have served to both comfort and, perhaps, somehow sustain him as he entered that frightening stage of his life. Clearly, it has had a lasting impression on Maurice and continues to do so some eighty years later.

***

Shortly after the young boy received the sandwiches from his father he boarded a train bound for Northampton—alone. His short-lived childhood was about to come crashing down around him and his young life would never be the same again.

CHAPTER FOUR

THE TOWN OF NORTHAMPTON

Nestled upon the banks of the meandering River Nene, some 65 miles northwest of London in the agricultural East Midlands region of Central England lays the historic town of Northampton. Granted its first town charter by His Majesty King Richard I in 1189, Northampton boasts a very rich history. Archaeological findings indicate Northampton's early settlement as far back as the Bronze Age. It was the construction of Northampton Castle during the Middle Ages that put the heretofore obscure town "on the map," as it were. In its heyday, the castle served both as a "home away from home" for the Royal Family (when they grew weary of life in London) as well as a meeting place for sessions of Parliament. Outrageously, the venerable old castle was eventually demolished to make room for the construction of a railway station.

In addition to its numerous churches and monasteries founded during medieval times, the town lays claim to the University

This gate, now part of the railway station is all that remains of Northampton Castle

of Northampton.[44] History also records two separate "Battles of Northampton"—one in 1264 and the other in 1460. In the mid-seventeenth century's English Civil War Northampton sided with Parliament against King Charles II resulting in the destruction of the town walls and most of the castle. Later in that century, the Great Fire of Northampton destroyed most of the town.[45]

With the advent of the industrial development in the 18th century, the town was rebuilt and entered a period of rapid growth with the construction of the Grand Union Canal and the railroads in the 19th century—setting the groundwork for the town's status as Britain's industrial capital of footwear and leather manufacturing—a trade which dates back to the reign of the Tudors.[46]

***

This shoe-making, industrial Northampton was the scary new world seven-year-old Maurice entered as he stepped off the in-bound from London train filled with its precious cargo of children evacuees in the early autumn of 1939—wearing his

---

44 Stuart E. Prall and David H. Wilson, *A History of England Volume I: Prehistory to 1714* (Fort Worth: Holt, Rinehart and Winston, Inc., 1991), 127.
45 Ibid., 196.
46 W. G. Hoskins, *Provincial England: Essays in Social and Economic History* (London: Macmil- lan and Company Ltd., 1965), 78-81.

government-issued name label, and toting nothing but a small suitcase, a gas mask and just, perhaps, the remnants of a sandwich in his pocket.

What time of year was it when you got on that train?

I think it was the autumn. Let's see, yes. I'll never forget the walk from the school to the train station. And my father putting the sandwich in my pocket. It was just a normal train, a standard train. It ran from that station. And I forget how long I was on the train, but I know when we got to our destination I remember going into a hall, like a community hall, and we were all sitting down, feeling a bit tired, and people came in the hall and began pointing to certain children, me included. And they were selecting who they would like to take and live with them.

And your parents didn't know . . .

Didn't know where we were. Yes, and I remember hearing…"I'll take this one, and I'll take that one." And I found out that I was in Northampton, northeast of London. And it must be about sixty miles. Sixty to 100. Far enough to get away from the bombing. I was alone. I didn't know what was going on. Especially at that age—you didn't realize what's going on.

So what do you remember about the couple that selected little seven-year-old Maurice?

Not a lot really—this husband and wife. And I don't know whether they had any children as well. There's little I remember of that time—of our first evacuation. In actual fact, I think at one stage, there was a German plane came over the town.

I think…if my memory goes back. But I don't remember a lot about that time. The main thing is…I wanted to get home to my parents.

How long were you with those people?

Under six months. May have even been three months. Because I was so unhappy being away from my parents. I wasn't there long, but I always remember it because the school I went to. One play-time, I fell over and cut my knee, or cut on top of my knee, and it left a scar. And that scar is still there. I'll always remember that.

You were there for approximately three months, and you were homesick, and you ended up back in London with your parents?

Right.

You told me once that you were probably in five different homes?

In total, yes. Because I was in Northampton, Somerset, Fishguard. Tring, with my mother, and Kings Langley. I went to quite a few places. I think after first getting back, things seemed to quiet down a bit. And I went back to school then.

This was during the phony war before the bombing started in the summer of 1940 anticipating?

Right. What was going to happen? What could happen?

* * *

Maurice joined the exodus of thousands upon thousands of children who made their way back to their homes during the early winter of 1940. The bombing raids nearly everyone in Britain anticipated never came. Things had indeed quieted down, and with new guarded hope a somewhat normalized family life resumed back in East Hackney for Maurice and his parents. Then, in the spring of 1940 Hitler cranked-up his war machine once again, this time turning westward toward the Low Countries and Germany's long-time enemy: France.

Shortly after the bulk of the British Expeditionary Force narrowly slipped out of the clutches of the Nazi juggernaut during the so-called "Miracle at Dunkirk," the new threat of a landed invasion was added to the existing danger of aerial bombardment. This precipitated Pied Piper's second wave of evacuations. With that, in the early summer of 1940 seven-year-old Maurice and his five-year-old cousin Evelyn were evacuated together, to the picturesque county of Somerset in the southwest of England.

CHAPTER FIVE

SOMERSET COUNTY

Somerset is a mostly rural county of rolling hills in South West England, steeped in history, legends, and rich traditions of folk music, song, and dance. One of the most compelling places to visit is the town of Bath, known for its natural hot springs, and its original Roman Baths which also include ancient statues and a temple constructed in 60–70 AD.[47] Somerset County's Glastonbury lays claim to the oldest above-ground Christian church in the world, as well as Glastonbury Abbey whose monks (as legend has it), discovered the bones

of King Arthur and his beloved Queen Guinevere. As if that were not enough, there is the matter of the legendary visit by

---

47 Stephen Bird and Barry W. Cunliffe, The Essential Roman Baths (London: Scala Books, 2007), 1-47.

Joseph of Arimathea, who in AD 63 brought along no less than the "Holy Grail" of Monty Python lore.[48]

An expression of sudden recall (almost as though he was experiencing an epiphany of sorts) appeared on Maurice's face as he continued . . .

The next time I was sent to Somerset. And that I can remember more of. Because my cousin Evelyn, she was two years

Maurice with cousin Evelyn and his mother Cissy in Somerset

younger than me. And her parents spoke with my parents that it would be good if we both went together, went to the same place, and if we could live together. We decided, our parents decided that when you go into the hall to be selected, that if one of us is picked, the other one is not picked by the same people, she should start crying, because she wanted to be with me. And I always remember sitting on a chair in this hall and being selected. No, I was not selected. She was selected. And she started crying. And the only way they could pacify her was to take me as well. And I'll always remember, the husband said, "Oh, all right, we'll take him as well."

And it seemed that this couple who selected us was wealthy. And they had a large farm in Somerset. And it was the biggest farm in the area. It even had electrified fencing, to keep the

---

48 Stuart E. Prall and David H. Willson, A History of England Volume I: Prehistory to 1714 (Fort Worth: Holt, Rinehart and Winston, Inc., 1991), 1.

animals in individual fields. I'll always remember that. And he was in the Home Guard. He was an officer in the Home Guard. I remember one room was the armory in his house, where there were rifles and all that a Home Guard would have. The Home Guard was where the men volunteered to make certain if there was any damage to the house they would look after the rescue of the people if they're still in their homes. If there was any parachutist, German parachutist, they would look after the capture. I have a little remembrance of that particular stay in Somerset. Somerset was on the west of England. And the Germans attacked, bombed a nearby city, I forget the name of it now.

On the 14ᵗʰ of May, 1944, in his first speech to the nation as Secretary of State for War on BBC radio, Anthony Eden made a call to arms to the countless "ordinary" citizens of Great Britain, especially those who were not eligible to serve in the regular forces. This appeal was made in response to the "parachute menace" facing the British Isles as they braced for a German invasion, part of which would most certainly come from the air. The response was immediate with between 300,000-400,000 volunteers putting down their names. They were charged with the defense of the nearly 5,000 miles of British coastline in the event of the aforementioned German invasion. Eden named this new citizen force: "The Local Defense Volunteers" who later became more commonly known as the "Home Guard."[49]

* * *

And there were lots of things. We had to abide by the rules of the house. We never ate with them. We always ate in the kitchen. They ate in the dining room with their friends, whom they would invite. But we always ate in the kitchen.

---

49 S. P. Mackenzie, The Home Guard (Oxford: Oxford University Press, 1995), 34-35.

Did they have other children?

No. And the first day we were sent to school we were told to go out the front gate of the house and turn right, and follow, walk to school down that road. And I'll always remember we came around the bend and there were cows in the field looking over the fence of the field and that frightened us because we'd never seen a cow before. And we ran home. We ran home. We said we can't go down that road because there's animals. And they makes funny noises and we were taken by car, to the school. We were frightened of the cows.

You had never seen one before?

No. Especially up close. Living in London, where would you see a cow? Maybe in the butcher shop? And then I was unhappy. And the husband didn't get on too well with me. And we had some good times because I was with my cousin Evelyn. She always used to chase me. And I think I told you…well, one day my cousin was chasing me in the farmyard, and to get away from her, I ran into the milking shed. Now the milking shed consists of a long building and the cows used to come in one end of the building… and go into these stalls, which were set like herringbone* [50]And whenever a cow wanted to relieve itself it sprayed outwards, and it went crap. I came in I saw the rear ends of the cows. And so I said, oh, if they want to go to do a crap or anything I'll go around by their heads because we had a walkway around their heads. So I pivoted on my right foot to make a right, and unfortunately, that was where all the waste had been swept up from the early morning milking. And I was covered in shit. I was taken into the house

50 An arrangement consisting of rows of short, slanted, parallel lines.

and I had to go straight to bed. But first I went to the bathroom and had a bath, and then went straight to bed.

And another thing is, in the back of the house, there were also chickens. But the chickens were running loose, and some of the older boys who lived there used to come to this farm and play. And there were some children who were there before we were there. So they knew a lot about the area, more than us.

Were they evacuees also?

Yes. And I always remember what they used to do. They used to kill the chickens. But they used to kill the chickens with spikes. They used to get ahold of…there were these spikes in the ground. And what they used to do is grab a spike, and when the chicken was there, they would throw it at the chicken, so they spiked the chicken and killed it. I'll always remember that. They were mischievous.

And these were boys from London too, do you reckon?

Yes. I remember one stage. The Germans landed some of their troops nearby. Somerset. On West Country. They landed some troops there, and all the Home Guard were all rounded up and went out to that area, and that's all I know.

Paratroops?

I don't know. I know, as I said, the Germans had landed, and they had to send the Home Guard to capture them. And I didn't hear anything further. And lots of things happened there. But we were always separated from the norm. They wanted to keep their friends into the luxury of their own home. It seems that in

The "Cerebos Salt" label

England they not only owned this big farm, but they owned a big salt business. And it's called Cerebos Salt. Oh, yes, Cerebos Salt. And the tins of salt are in tins. And on the tin was a chicken running away from a boy with a can of salt, pointing and pouring on the back of the chicken. And I think, I wouldn't be surprised if that company is still in existence.

How long were you there, at this place?

About six months. Remember I…wherever I was sent, I never seemed to last long. Because I wanted to get back to London—to my parents. It was something one went through and a lot of things that were fine though. And being away from one's parents, one missed the love of your parents. Because at that age, obviously, you want it.

And as I told you, we never ate with the people who took us into their house to live with them. We always ate in the kitchen. And we had a nursery room in the house, in which we could play and talk. This is with Evelyn, my cousin. And one afternoon I remember looking out the window into the apple orchard, which was behind the house, lots of apple trees. So I said to Evelyn, "Fancy an apple?" And she said, "Yes, I do, but I'm not going out." And I said, "Well, I'll go out." And so I went along the hall, down the stairs, to the ground floor, out the back door into the orchard, and took quite an armful of apples. Came back in the house, this was in the back of the house, up the stairs to the first floor they had, back to the playroom. We used to call it a playroom. And then when I turned, I opened the door to the playroom, Evelyn was in there, and I turn around and ran in and closed the door, and as I closed the door, I looked through the doorway down the hall, and the house had light green carpet and it rained the night before. I never changed my shoes when I went out into the orchard. And all along the top hallway, in that hall, along the light green carpet, was my muddy footsteps...and down the stairs as well. I said to Evelyn, "I think I'm going to be in trouble." Later on in the afternoon, the wife came home, and then I could hear shouting downstairs. Then the shouting got louder. The wife was coming up the stairs with the husband. Next thing I knew the door opened, and the nurse...because we had a nurse...she says, "You're having a bath, I'm going to have to bathe you and you're going straight to bed." And that's what happened. And then they had to call a cleaner in to clean the carpet, going down the stairs. And she said to me why I didn't change my shoes because that was the rule? Whenever you went out of the house, you went to either the front door or the back door, you had shoes there. So you would change your shoes when you came into the house and put your slippers on. So that was a boo-boo that I made going to get some apples from the orchard.

The owner of the house was in the Home Guard, they had a Home Guard there, even though it was in the country. And he had a room in the house which was specifically for all equipment of the Home Guard. Guns, rifles, knives, stretchers. And I seem to remember, one night, they said that some German parachutist had dropped near. There was a whole hullabaloo. I was inquisitive one time, looking at his closed door, which went into this room. And then another time the door was left ajar. Nobody was there except me. So I walked in. I just saw the guns laying down, or standing up against the wall, and some of the things. And he came in and saw me, blew a top, and he had a gun in his hand and he hit me with it.

Hit you with a gun?

Yeah. None of it exploded, but it hit me. He was saying to me, "Don't you ever dare go in there again."

He should have kept it locked if it was that dangerous.

Well, you know, at a young age, the door's open, nobody's there, look around and you go in. And somehow I used to get on the telephone and then one weekend I heard that my cousin Evelyn, her father was coming down to see her, just as a visit. And one weekend my mother and Evelyn's mother came down to see us. And they finished up that he, more or less, the people we were with told him how unhappy I was, that he then took me home.

This was your uncle?

Yes.

Were you close to him?

Not really.

They took you both?

No, they never took her. They left Evelyn there.

But as I say, when Evelyn's father left on Sunday to go home, back to London, he took me. And I was back in London again. I was happy...I was back in London again.

* * *

Maurice's stay in London turned out to be an abbreviated one, certainly not for as long as the young boy had hoped. For, when his uncle brought him home in the late fall of 1940, it was the worst of all possible times, a time in which the Battle of Britain was reaching its zenith in terms of the intensity and frequency of the Luftwaffe's nightly bombing raids. (Maurice describes his harrowing experiences with "the Blitz" in a subsequent chapter) These nightly raids were becoming so intense that his mother, Sissy decided it was time to get her son out of London once again—this time accompanied by herself. In the early winter of 1941, Maurice reluctantly said goodbye to his father, clasped his mother's hand, and boarded yet another train filled with his fellow "refugees"—this time, bound for Wales and the fishing village of Fishguard.

CHAPTER SIX

THE VILLAGE OF FISHGUARD

Seated in a deep valley, where the River Gwaun meets the sea, lies the quiet Welsh fishing village of Fishguard. Of historical significance, Fishguard was the site of the last invasion of mainland Britain. In February of 1797, the newly formed French revolutionary government devised a plan that aimed to gain the sympathy of the poor country folk of Britain in support of their revolutionary "call to liberty." A ramshackle French invading force was assembled and proceeded to land at Fishguard, Pembrokeshire. Soon after

Gastineau, Henry G., 1791-1876
Adlard, H. (Henry), fl. 1828-1869

debarkation, they commandeered a large cache of French whiskey and became terribly intoxicated—almost to a man.

The invaders were subsequently subdued and humiliatingly forced to surrender to an under-armed, out-numbered, and quite astonished troop of Welsh militia—a rather inglorious end to the last invasion of England.[51]

Fishguard's roots can be traced back to the era of the Vikings in the tenth century when the terrified people of coastal Wales were oft subjected to the fury of the fierce Norse raiders.[52] Impressed with the natural harbors and bountiful fishing waters, these sea-faring invaders from the north eventually established trading posts and settlements in the region. The Village of Fishguard was one such settlement. It was to this picturesque village by the sea that Maurice and his mother traveled, seeking sanctuary from an even deadlier raider. Unlike their tenth century counterparts, these twentieth-century raiders did not arrive out of the north, by sea. They came out of the south, by air—from across the English Channel—to deposit their fiery hell upon the terrified people of London, out of the black night sky.

Maurice sat up in his chair, cleared his throat and continued...

And then they came out with a decision to include mothers with their children in the evacuation process. And that was the

---

51 James Baker, A Brief Narrative of the French Invasion,Near Fishguard Bay: Including a Perfect Description of that Part of the Coast of Pembrokeshire, on which was Affected the Landing of the French Forces, on the 22nd of February, 1797, and of Their Surrender to the Welch Provincial Troops, Headed by Lord Cawdor. By J. Baker, author of the Picturesque Guide through Wales and the Marches. [Worcester]: Printed for the author, by J. Tymbs, at the Cross, Worcester, 1797. Eighteenth Century Collections Online. Gale. Indiana University Library, South Bend. 19 Nov. 2016. http://find.galegroup.com.proxysb.uits.iu.edu/ ecco/ infmark.do?&source=gale&prodId=ECCO&userGroupName=iulib_sbend&tabID=T001&d cId=C-   B127705935&type=multipage&contentSet=ECCOArticles&version=1.0&docLevel FACSIMILE.
52 B. G. Charles, The Placenames of Pembrokeshire (Aberystwyth: National Library of Wales, 1992), 50.

first time my mother came away with me. And again we had to meet at the local railway station. Where we were going? Nobody knew. When would we get there? Nobody knew. What we had to do is to make certain you had your gas mask around your shoulder or around your head. It was in a cardboard box. And we all got on this train that came in, and this left about 9 o'clock in the morning, and the train pulled out. We were on the train at lunchtime still. The train was still going. Not fast, but going slowly. And then some of us found out that we would not get to our destination that day, but we were going to Wales. And the first night we were going to stay in a hospital, have a bath, have dinner. And we'd be going on to our destination the next day. And we got to the hospital...well, we got to a station. We didn't know where it was. And again we were taken to a hospital and were told we would be given breakfast in the morning, and then we'd be taken back to the railway station on the journey to where we were going. And our mothers got together and said, "Why have we got to get on the train the next day to go to our destination? Can't we stay another night because we were tired from the journey that day?" They said, "You can't, you've got to carry on the next day." Next day we got up, had breakfast, they added buses which took us from the hospital to the station, and we continued our journey. That night, the second night...the Germans bombed that hospital.

Oh, my God. What city was that?

Fishguard. Near Fishguard. On the coast. The village. My mother and I were together obviously, evacuated with a spinster, and she had something go wrong with her. She had a twisted face, and she just scared me. And I always remember she used to do the washing in a tub, and hang the washing up in the kitchen on boards.

And the mothers, when we used to go out weekends for walks, we used to walk down to the beach, and walking down to the beach along the country lanes there were brooks and streams running alongside the road, and in the streams was watercress. And on the beach, there was a guard, an older man, and he was a guard to see that nothing went wrong. And I always remember my mother saying to him, "What would you do if a German boat came along and landed some people?" So my mother said, "Do you have a telephone?" He actually said he would run back to the village and report it. And my mother said, "If you go back to the beach, that's about two or three miles walk. You're taking a long time." He said, "Oh, that's all we got."

Apparently, the government decided that it was cruel and inhumane to deprive these little kids of the love that they were obviously missing out on. Do you think that's why they let the moms come along?

Well, the children were missing their parents and the mothers were missing their children.

There was an outcry?

Mm-hm. Well, it was all so new…all these different arrangements. And obviously the people you were staying at had to be paid. You couldn't do it for nothing. Also, the food was rationed at that time. You were only allowed one or two eggs a week. Any fruit came from abroad, you couldn't get. An orange was like gold because they never grew in England.

A lot happened. But I had more experiences from then on being in London, because being evacuated the last time to Wales, I was sent away with my mother or another member of the family closer to London, which wasn't bombed.

Do you remember much about Wales? What it was like staying in that place?
Well, it was like a basic village. And every storekeeper or shopkeeper was related to each other. So if you fell out with one storekeeper you fell out with two or three others. One thing I always remembered was that when my mother would go shopping with me, we would go into a particular store and you saw those other people there, and when they saw us come in, they started speaking Welsh. So the mothers couldn't understand what they were talking about and could be talking about them. So the Jewish mothers replied, not replied, but started talking between themselves in Yiddish. So that was the situation there.

Were the Jewish mothers from London?
Yes. No Jewish mothers there.

What kind of a house was it?
It was a one-story house if I remember. I always remember the kitchen, or we say dining room now, on the ceiling you had a construction where she used to hang her washing to dry. And you could higher it or lower it, to lower things on to it or to take things off of it. Another thing in Wales, we were fairly close to the beach. And I remember many of us walking to the beach, you were walking on a country road, you had a brook one side, a stream, and in

that stream, there was watercress growing. And my mother said to pick it because you can eat it. And there was an island just off the beach and there was housing there on this island, and one of the houses on the island was owned by the woman we were staying with, her relationship. And my mother got on well with her. But you could only go there when it was low tide. Walkout to it. When the tide was high you couldn't go there.

Did most of the kids have their mothers? Did any of them go with their fathers, aunts or sisters?
No.

Was there a big fear of invasion?
Well, they did try to raid. You know that, don't you? Oil. Put it on fire. Well, this is mainly on the South Coast of England about 100 yards off the beach. There were pipes showing above the water level. These pipes, it was probably round about five foot, six-foot-high, above the surface. And these pipes, we found this out after the war, these pipes were connected onshore to a building and then the Germans collected and loaded some small boats, and one night they decided to get going and see if they could land on the East Coast of England.

The East Coast?
No, sorry, the South Coast. And next thing was known was a liquid was coming out of these pipes. And then it was lit alight. And this was only lit alight once the German boats were passing- in other words, between the pipes and the beach. So the Germans were caught in these flames and they had to reverse and go back.

And they said, this was reported in the papers, that the Germans had to get emergency transportation trains on the North French Coast to take the wounded back to Germany.

The story of Great Britain's petroleum-fueled defeat of a German invasion force off the South coast of England in 1940 was ultimately one of the greatest myths to come out of World War II. This myth was, in fact, so popular that a book was written about it in 2001 by the author James Hayward entitled: "The Bodies on the Beach—Sea Lion, Shingle Street and the Burning Sea Myth of 1940." Indeed, experiments with floating petroleum on the sea and igniting it did take place, yet their success was limited as the fuel was difficult to ignite, large quantities were required to cover even the smallest of areas and the process was easily disrupted by waves. This defense method did show potential, however prompting the development of a flame barrage technique in 1941. This technique eliminated the old method which attempted to ignite oil floating on water. Instead, nozzles were placed above high-water mark with pumps producing sufficient pressure to spray fuel-producing an impressive wall of flame over, rather than on, the water. Although this weapon was impressive, its network of pipes was vulnerable to pre-landing bombardment—prompting its initially ambitious plans to be cut back to cover just a few miles of beaches. [53]

***

Germany's bombing campaign finally came to an end in May 1941 as Hitler redirected his aggression toward the Soviet Union. The conclusion of this initial phase of the Battle of Britain saw a three-year lull in hostilities on the home front, with a much needed

---

53 James Hayward, The Bodies On The Beach—Sea Lion, Shingle Street and the Burning Sea Myth of 1940 (Norfolk: CD41 Publishing, 2001), 21-25.

reprieve for the government of Great Britain and her people. But this was only a temporary reprieve, as we shall later see. This nation-wide "all clear" allowed Maurice to return home to East Hackney for the third time in one and one-half years. Indeed, over the course of the war, the young lad spent as much time living at home as his parents would allow—providing him with a plethora of experiences to pass down to future generations, while at the same time exposing him to dangers that we can only try to imagine. So, let us now return our focus once again to East Hackney, and discover what life was like for Maurice between evacuations.

CHAPTER SEVEN

EAST HACKNEY AT WAR

After coming back from Somerset I spent quite a bit of time in London. So I was involved with the bombing. And I stayed in London for quite a long time when the raids started. And my memory is of my mother waking me up in the middle of the night, with the warning sounding, and taking me into the shelter in the garden, or the community shelter down bottom of the street. Yes, Anderson Shelter. The government built these shelters in your garden. Didn't cost you anything. And it housed probably about four bunks, two on either side. They excavated the ground, they dug a big hole in the ground, must have been about from that wall to about the end of that table. And then it was put in the ground, and the soil that was taken out to put it in the soil was then put on top of it. It wouldn't have survived a direct hit. We'd be woken up in the middle of the night with an air raid warning, and then my mother gathering me and quickly putting some clothes on me, grabbing me by the hand and pulling me, rushing me down to the community shelter.

How many blocks, was it a long run?
I would imagine that it was probably about a quarter of a mile.

How did she know to go there, as opposed to your Andersen shelter?
Well, the air raids, whenever there was one in the evening, it used to last most of the night. And to stay in the Andersen shelter

all night we would be tired, cold, depending on the weather. If it was pouring rain, you'd be wet in there. So my mother was going to the community shelter. It consisted of lots of rooms. It was a big furniture store.

And they arranged the basement to be different rooms, and put bunks in these rooms. And in its construction, there were lots of rooms, and they built bunk beds in each of the rooms. And there-

fore I think you were allocated a particular room to go through, your family. And therefore you got friendly with the people who also were in that room. And I remember it was all brick construction. There was one connecting corridor. And I don't know how they constructed this because it was built before the war to have this big area with all these rooms. But my mother, a normal night when the raids were on, used to start 'round about 10 o'clock.

Your father wouldn't leave the house?

No, he wouldn't go into the shelter. He said, "If they're going to kill me, kill me in my house." And he wouldn't go in the shelter.

To erect one of these Andersen shelters was a formidable job, indeed. First, a hole 7.5 feet long by 6 feet wide was dug to a depth of 4 feet. In this hole, 6 curved steel sheets were inserted and bolted together—forming an arch. At either end were steel plates—one which could be unbolted to provide an emergency exit. There was also a hole at ground level

A woman hangs the wash above her family's Anderson Shelter

through which one could climb down into or out of the shelter. Outside, the shelter was covered with no less than 15 inches of earth. It should come as no surprise that some Londoners said it felt rather like being entombed in a small, dark bicycle shed, smelling of earth and damp.[54]

Were there others with your father's attitude?

No. None that I know of. He was something. He wouldn't do it. And we were close to where the bombs were falling—incendiary bombs, land mines. But the one time that we nearly all got killed was I told you...when he told us to come out of the shelter to have a hot cup of tea in the house. I told you that, didn't I? We were sitting around the fire, talking. This must have been about

---

54 Norman Longmate, How We Lived Then: A History of Everyday Life during the Second World War (London: Hutchinson and Company Publishers Ltd., 1971), 121-122.

2 o'clock in the morning. And suddenly, boom. All the windows come in, dust and things moved. And it was a mine. The Germans were dropping mines on parachutes. So you didn't know, you couldn't hear them coming down. And if it was windy, they would blow until they hit a draft and...next day my mother was up to school to get me evacuated.

Months later, Maurice related that this was the closest he and his family had come to dying during the war. He further confided with me that when that mine exploded—blowing out his house's windows—he called out to the heavens for God to spare his young life—something, he admits, he has not done since.

***

And our garden, assuming I was sitting in the kitchen, in the shelter now, we had a railway line running this way, on an embankment, and another railway running that way. And the Germans always used to aim for the intersection of this railway and that railway. Because they could put them out of action. And this railway line would have an anti-aircraft gun on a carriage, and the locomotive that was pulling it would go up and down, and sometimes they used to fire off at German planes. And that railway used to run north and south and a lot of the Allied troops in the invasion of France would always be on that railway, going down towards the sea. Yes, and I used to wave to the troops in the garden. Lots of memories.

And then we started getting the V-1s, and we used to go to the shelter in our garden. And our house was at the corner of two railway lines. I think I explained that. There used to be an

Ack-ack[*55] gun on a trailer. And the locomotive used to pull it along. And I can hear it now. It was a Pom Pom.

"Pom-Pom" anti-aircraft gun mounted on a rail car

Was it parked right by your backyard?

Yes. And being in the shelter, the Anderson shelter, in our garden, it was so loud. Because the Pom Pom gun[†] [56]and locomotive was on the rail, it moves up and down this line. But I'll always remember the poom poom poom—it was so loud.

What about the other rail line?

That was mainly a passenger line. And many times there used to be the army being moved from one region to the next or they were changing where they were staying or doing. And I always remember the troops or the army hanging out the windows, waving away as they went past.

How often did you talk to your father when you were away with your mom?

Rare, rare. Because he was a tailor so he was at work and out of work. He was always looking to get a job. So it was my mother

---

55 A nickname used for "anti-aircraft" guns derived from the phonetic alphabet used by the British for the voice transmission of "AA."

56 A type of automatic, rapid-firing, small-caliber anti-aircraft cannon used in World War II.

who took the lead. But when he decided to open this greengrocery shop, he got more involved with everything. He used to get up at 4:30 in the morning to the market to buy goods to be sold that day. Potatoes, all the different…tomatoes, everything you could think of in a greengrocers shop.

Where was the shop?
Hackney.

Where was the market he went to?
Covent Garden. And when I came back to London, a couple of times, he used to take me to the market. And he used to have breakfast at the market because it was too early to have breakfast at home. And one of the things he would say, it was jellied eels. Have you heard of that? Yeah, eels cooked. Yes, I remember eating jellied eels. And then because it wasn't just plain buying at the market, because you had things that were rationed. You could only have…like oranges were rarely for sale. And then they were rationed. So various other fruits were rationed that you got from abroad. You hardly got anything coming in from abroad because boats were being sunk by the Germans. Yes, certain things come to mind at different times. And I always remember the night we nearly got killed. You know, with that bomb. I think the next day, or the day after that, my mother got us evacuated. Because at that period, it was after sunset, she was happy with just taking me to the shelters. But that being so close.

…The Americans used to have a restaurant up in the West End. You know where the West End is, don't you?

I've been there.

Rainbow Corner, it used to be called. And the Americans used to meet there. There was always something going on there.

By D-Day, the American Red Cross effort in Great Britain had reached its zenith with some 2,000 American personnel on staff, and an additional 500 in hospital service. The organization also directed 10,000 paid British employees along with a further 13,000 civilian volunteers. It boasted some 265 clubs of varying sizes in operation—the largest being "Rainbow Corner" near London's famous Piccadilly Circus, which was designed largely to cater to GIs on leave. The club was open to American servicemen 24 hours a day, 365 days a year from 11 November, 1942 to 9 January, 1946.[57]

***

We continued...

Do you remember the rubble in the morning the day after? Do you remember the ruins? What was that like?

Yes. It was just a mound of bricks and mortar and wood. Where everything had collapsed and been blown apart.

Winston Churchill surveys the damage after a German air raid

---

57 Norman Longmate, The GIs: The Americans in Britain 1942-1945 (New York: Charles Scribner's Sons, 1975), 131.

How often did Churchill go on the radio?

I don't think there was a specific time that he went on the radio. Just maybe after some big place had been bombed, and he'd gone down to view it. Then he would make some remarks on the radio. But it wasn't a weekly event.

Were there people trying to rescue people?

At the time I was looking at was in the daylight. Those other people were there in the night. Like my father mostly at night helping. They had what they called Home Guard. And these are private people trained to help survivors put out fires. I remember my father when he joined the Home Guard going to a lesson on using a stirrup pump. It's a pump that you pump water. And it comes out in a pipe. And if an incendiary bomb caught a house alight or something like that, the Home Guard used to help put the fire out, because the fire brigade was so overwhelmed with work with big buildings and everything outside of the normal small houses. That's how they're being helped by the Home Guard. But also you had to be careful of the flying shrapnel when the bomb explodes. And part of the bomb is metal. It flies and injures a lot of people. A lot used to go on at night where the Home Guard were in the midst of it.

Didn't the Home Guard also capture downed pilots?

Well, that does happen. It happened. That fighter plane that they brought down. They arrested the pilot.

And I remember one night a bomb was dropped. They tried to defuse it. They failed, and two or three people of the Army were in a crater. They all were killed.

Did you see that?

Saw the after effect. Also remember, the V-1s and the V-2s. The V-2, the rockets—them coming down. This was towards the end of the war. The Germans were using the V-2 rockets. And I remember being ill, I was at home by that time. And I was in bed, and suddenly there was an almighty explosion. A V-2 rocket landed fairly close to our area, Hackney. And a whole lot of people killed.

It woke you up?

No, I think I was up. Just in bed. What also happened there, you know, the V-1s. The buzz bombs. After they were in use for some time, the Royal Air Force got used to turning them around in flight. What they used to do on the wings, the end of the wing, a Spitfire would come up and it would fly alongside it, and the Spitfire pilot would move his plane so his wingtip touched the wingtip of the buzz bomb and turned it 'round to come back the way it came.

But where would it go? Over the channel and just land in the sea?

Right. And one of my uncles was in the Army. He was on the anti-aircraft guns. What the Army did, they positioned loads of anti-aircraft guns in a semicircle around the bottom of London. The Southern part of London, in a curve. So when these German planes used to come in from the South, they formed like a line of guns to fire at them. And quite a few of them used to be down.

Did you ever see a German plane flying over?

Yes. Well, you were frightened, and you were being moved or pushed by other people. At night. I still remember the first

V-1 that came over London. I remember I was in the bedroom, and the warning had sounded, and everyone could hear it, and suddenly it's engine stopped. The following morning, the question was, "What was it?" So the Army said, "They shot the plane down and the engine—the shells must have hit the engine to stop it." But that wasn't true. Just one ran out of fuel. Then they dived down. That's how these occurred. I think a lot of the time they were concentrating on the docks, because London … the Thames, when you went through London, there were lots of companies, manufacturing war material that were located in the dock area, along the Thames. And that's where the Germans were aiming at putting their action. They were lucky St. Paul's was never hit – St. Paul's Church. But I remember going to my parents, putting me to sleep, and then I just fell asleep obviously, then the air raid warning would sound, and my mother would come into my bedroom, dress me, and take me, if we were going to the communal shelter, rushing through the street, Graham Road, and I remember I could see the picture of the entrance to the community shelter, which was in a back street, and going along a small side street to get to the back street, they built a shelter in brick in the road. So like a surface shelter.

Is this the furniture store?

No, it was going to it. You had to go through a side street to get to the furniture store.

And in this side street they built a brick shelter, just above …not dug into the ground, it was just on top. It was like a glass shelter. There's lots of things one remembers, and you know, as you get older your memory shows you, as if you're looking at it. I can see it.

It's that vivid, is it?
So vivid.

When did you return to London for good? No more evacuations?
When we came back from Tring. That was, well, I was just under 13. Well, it'd be '44.

Maurice's written memoirs show him actually returning home from Kings Langley in early 1945. Recently, he verified this with me in a conversation we had at a father's day cook-out at his home over some amazing beef burgers and kosher hot dogs he grilled himself.

* * *

They realized using planes to bomb, it was just a certain period they used planes. They were finding that the Air Force and the Spitfires were good at bringing down their planes. Therefore, they were looking for other items they could use. And that's when they started off with the V-1. And when they found England got over the V-1s, you know the buzz bombs, they looked for something else, where they didn't lose so many lives, especially when they started using rockets.

Operational from 1938 to 1954, Britain's single-seat Spitfire fighter plane was one of the most renown and elegant aircraft in aviation history. When the plane's prototype first flew in March of

1936, it appeared so small and fast that a senior German officer dismissed it, contemptuously, as 'a toy'. He could not have been more mistaken. The Spitfire was armed with four 0.303 Browning machine guns, four 20 mm cannons and could carry 1000 lbs. of bombs or rockets. This highly maneuverable fighter could reach a top speed of 454 mph, with a rate of climb by 80 percent. Used as an interceptor during the Battle of Britain, this phenomenal airplane shared victory over Germany's Luftwaffe with its capable counterpart, the Hurricane. When production ceased in 1947, the grand total of all Spitfires produced tallied 20,351.[58]

* * *

But there was a lull, of a couple of years, right?

Yes, but they were bombing other areas. And they were in the country. Birmingham, they used to bomb, Manchester, because that was where a lot of the British munitions were manufactured. Coventry. It was dying down. Because when they first started evacuating children it was mainly from London. Because that's where they thought Hitler would concentrate all their bombers. Bomb London and the British people would give up.

Didn't work, did it?

It didn't.

You talked about the train that went North and South, and the one that went East and West. And you'd see soldiers waving to you? Was this around '44?

---

58 John Keegan, The Rand McNally Encyclopedia of World War II, ed. S. L. Mayer (Chicago: Rand McNally & Company, 1977), 226.

Yes, they were going to Europe. I'll always remember waving to them, and them waving back. Because there's a lot of American troops in England, they had a club in the West End, Piccadilly Circus. And I remember the corner it was on—Over the Rainbow Club. And they used to have parties there, and every night the Yanks were there.

Did they give you candy or anything?

Oh, yes, we used to go and ask them for gum. "Got any gum, Chum?" Because it was the Americans that made chewing gum popular. And all the American soldiers all seemed to have plenty of gum in their pockets. "Got any gum, Chum?"

Did you "chum around" with other kids in London when you were getting gum from the Yank?

Maurice and his parents at his Bar Mitzvah

I was with a few friends. I had a couple of good friends. One was named Segal. Another one was called Jerry. But it wasn't tight relationships.

But yes, so I came back to London. Just before 12. Because I remember at 13 my parents wanted me to go have a Bar Mitzvah. And I had no bringing up being Jewish. So I had to go to a Rabbi twice a week. And there was a collection of boys all training for their Bar Mitzvahs. And it took me six months to do my training.

And I got Bar Mitzvahed the same time as one of my friends. So we were both on the Bimah*[59] together.

What was the training like? At the Shul?
No, at the house of the Rabbi. He had a long table, and we used to sit around the table, and he used to teach us to read Hebrew.

Had you not been evacuated, you would have started learning Hebrew when you were nine?
Much earlier.

So the war interrupted your religious upbringing as well as your social life, your family life and everything else.
Right.

What was the food like?
Food was limited. You had rationing of food—eggs, meat—certain fruits. Hardly saw an orange. And you had a ration book. And when you bought your...you're only allowed a certain amount of each per week. And when you bought it, they mark your ration book. You can't get any more that week. Milk, eggs, meat, certain fruits, can't remember what else.

On a typical day, what would you eat?
Well, bread, you use to make yourself. Egg, if you had an egg. Rice...corn flakes.

Did your mom keep kosher? Talk about her a little.
Well, my mother was one of thirteen children. My grandfather on that side, it was his second marriage. And my mother's first

---

59 The podium in front of a synagogue where the "Torah" is read.

marriage. My mother was the oldest of the … my mother was the first child to be born to the marriage of my grandfather and her. And the first…my grandfather was married before in Poland, on my mother's side. When he came to England, he married my grandmother. Her first child was my mother. This is the second marriage. And then my mother had to do all the work with the remaining children that were home. She had to do their washing in the cellar. She has to cook—do the cooking for the other younger children. She worked pretty hard. And she helped in the butcher shop when she was a lot older. When she got married to my father, she used to help occasionally in the butcher shop. Which the butcher shop was run by my grandmother, the second grandmother, and the boys were still going to school. My uncles. And when my mother got married, my father was out of work most of the time, it was the war, she used to help in the butcher shop. But they were hard times. They were hard times, I tell you, those.

And you were poor too.

Yes, we were. My father used to have unemployment at times. And that's how people lived then.

So, you had to go back to school then when you came home?

Yes, I went to another school in another area. I walked there. And I remember one day coming out seeing the gliders going over. Well, that morning they rumored that the Allies had landed in Europe. And I went to school as usual. And I used to come home for lunch, or go to my grandma's for lunch, in the butcher shop. Because my mother was helping in the butcher shop in the morning. So I used to go there for lunch and coming out you could hear the planes, and you looked up, and all these squadrons had planes towing gliders, were all heading in a southerly direction.

Were they American planes, or British planes?

Both. I think that the gliders were called Norseman or something like that.

On June 5ᵗʰ, 1944 (D-day "minus-one") the roar of hundreds of aircraft engines could be heard over London and the surrounding towns and villages of southern and central England. As a powerful air armada passed over their homes, farms, and workplaces, thousands of British subjects turned their attention skyward— marveling at the sights and sounds of three British and American airborne divisions that took to the air in over 1,200 aircraft. This unprecedented airborne assault on Normandy was spearheaded by D Company, 2nd Battalion of His Majesty's Oxfordshire and Buckinghamshire Light Infantry—flown in six Horsa gliders, which were towed by six Halifax bombers.[60] Operation Neptune, as it was code-named, marked the first time that British and American forces had used gliders in such a large-scale of combat operations—the R.A.F. deploying its Horsas, and the U.S. Army Air Corps transporting troops and personnel with their smaller "Waco" gliders. They could deliver fully loaded, ready to fight, combat troops to pin-point landing zones behind enemy lines—unlike their paratroop counterparts who were often scattered in their drops, requiring precious time to regroup and deploy. Gliders could also be mass-produced quite cheaply, and it was much easier (and less expensive) to train

---

60 Antony Beevor, D-DAY: The Battle for Normandy (New York: Viking, 2009), 51.

glider troops compared to paratroopers who were sent to a four-week "jump school." Despite these advantages, glider combat was extremely dangerous and unpredictable as gliders were unarmed, unarmored, and powerless to do anything but land (or crash) once cut-loose from their towing aircraft. Their short history was full of horror stories, prompting their vulnerable troops to coin them "flying coffins," and "towed targets."[61]

***

That's when I started getting interested in airplanes and going in for engineering. It's difficult being a certain age, knowing what to do, what training you need. My interest was building model airplanes, buy the balsa wood, and carving them. And then I went along to buying kits of flying aircraft.

This is during the war you did this?

At the end of it.

Did they recall soldiers from around the empire back to England in the case of the invasion?

No. Well, because Japan was starting. So they had to look after their colonists. Also, some of the British troops were sent to Egypt. My uncle, he went as part of the 8th Army. And he traveled...he was in the medical corps. And he was shipped to a big camp in Cairo. And he followed the movement of the 8th Army. So he went all along North Africa from Cairo to Tripoli. Then he went across to Sicily, and from Sicily into the toe of Italy.

---

61 Ed Ruggero, The First Men In: U.S. Paratroops and the Fight to Save D-Day (New York: HarperCollins Publishers, 2006), 50-51.

And then traveled North through Italy chasing the Germans. Yes, he must have had some stories.

I wanted to ask you about the Black Shirts.

The Black Shirts. Well, there was a big market in North Hackney, North of Hackney, and it was really crowded this market, and there were many stores—shops. And at one end, there's a big car park, where the Black Shirts used to hold their meetings. And it was always run by a guy named Moseley. And you found that the speakers were like standing on boxes so they were high up, and the crowd was all around them. And the police were there riding horses to keep the crowd behaving…to make the crowd behave themselves. And some of the Fascists there didn't like the horses. There used to be a horse along, on the road, obviously, their horses, step on them or step over. And it happened to me once when I was there, about from you to me, this horse, with a policeman on top riding it, came down on the floor next to me.

Did he hit you?

No, I was lucky. But after the war*62 they stopped the meetings. The police stopped the meetings, or the government. Moseley wouldn't speak anymore.

What was their platform? They were basically Nazis, right?

Yes. And it was probably about 500 people at least attending these meetings in the car park.

---

62 Maurice later correctly recalled that this could not have occurred "after the war" as the Blackshirts were banned from Britain in 1940—a rare and understandable mistake given the 76 years that had since passed.

How far was this from your house?

Two miles. Something like that. But I never used to go there specifically every time. It just happened once when we were at the market. We went into that end of the Market near the car park, and we saw the Fascists there. The police were there, as I say. But after the war, the Fascists disappeared. I was never there when they first met. The meetings – when I was there the meetings had already started.

The "Flash and Circle" flag of the British Union of Fascists.

They didn't wear swastikas, did they?

Yes.

Did they do any violent things?

Not that I know of, because that's why they had the police there. *Most historians would agree that British fascism was the personal creation of Sir Oswald Mosley. Although there were a few, for the most part, insignificant fascist movements in the 1920s, they were virtually extinct by the 1930s. That said, it is highly unlikely that a powerful fascist movement such as the British Union of Fascists (commonly known as the Black Shirts) would have developed in Britain during the 1930s were it not for Mosley, who gave the movement his prestige—which at that time was considerable. Growing British hostility towards Nazi Germany contributed to the decline of the movement's membership until it was finally banned by the British government in 1940, shortly after the start of the Sec-*

ond World War. Soon thereafter, a number of prominent Blackshirts were arrested and interned including Mosley himself.[63]

* * *

Do you remember when you first heard the news that the troops landed in France on D-Day?

I do remember it. And I remember it's all we would talk about before they went in, months before, and the Allies built dummy tanks to fool the Germans, where they were going to land.

I remember the Allies building the moorings on the French Coast, the boats would come and unload. In the morning you saw the planes coming over London—flying, heading south. And there was a lot more troops in the streets, but generally walking around.

Americans?

American, Canadian, I didn't see many French. No. The main ones I saw was Canadians, Americans, Australians.

And you saw the gliders come over one day.

Yes. What made it so good to see were these gliders being towed. I think the gliders were called Norsemen. But they had to be lucky with the weather with the gliders. Because once they were launched, that's it. And so they also have to be forewarned where they could land. In other words, places—not in trees. Because they only had a gliding path, and if they missed out, they passed, and probably all were killed. Then some months later, you

---

63 S. J. Woolf, European Fascism (New York: Random House Inc, 1968), 231.

had the Battle of the Bulge. Well, you know, you heard about the advancement of the Allied troops. And I think it was more the Allied troops until the Russians reached Berlin. And then it was more about the Russians, because they were in Berlin. I remember reading reports of the Allied help to the Russians, taking boats to the Russians on the North Sea. And what the people in the boats had to go through, the weather, the bad weather. You know the cold. To supply the Russians they used to launch the ships to Russia in the North of England and Scotland.

* * *

On the twelfth of June, 1944, just six days after the allies breached the defenses of Hitler's "Fortress Europe" establishing a beachhead at the coast of Normandy, Nazi Germany unleashed the first of its "vengeance weapons" upon the unsuspecting populations of South-East England, including the city of London. These deadly attacks by the pulse-jet propelled V-1 "buzz bombs" followed by the long-range V-2 rockets resulted in the third and the final wave of the evacuation of London's children. At a time when the war seemed to have been all but won Maurice and his mother were once again on the move, this time to a small town situated adjacent to an American airbase some 100 miles north of London, by the unlikely name of "Tring."

CHAPTER EIGHT

THE TOWN OF TRING

If a person was to travel through a certain gap in the Chiltern Hills, of West Hertfordshire, he or she would have the pleasure of encountering the beautiful market town of Tring. Throughout its history, Tring's most notable residents were arguably the Rothschilds—a wealthy Jewish family whose contributions and influence on the town since the late 19th century have been considerable—not the least of which is a private zoological museum that boasts the largest collection of stuffed animals in the world. Interestingly, Tring was also the home of John Washington who was the great-grandfather of George Washington, the first President of the United States.[64] During the Second World War Tring served as a way station of sorts for the personnel of an American airbase situated in the town's outskirts.[65] Perhaps, taking a

---

64 Murray Neil. "The Washingtons of Tring," Tring & District Local History & Museum Society, 2013.http://www.hertfordshire-genealogy.co.uk/data/books/books-6/book-0632-washingtons-of-tring.htm

65 Jill Fowler, Tring through Time (Gloucestershire: Amberley Publishing, 2009), 47.

cue from Germany's strategic script, it was from this base that Britain's American allies launched their daring daytime air raids over Germany in their own equally futile attempt to destroy the infrastructure and break the resolve of their enemy. Quid pro quo the cycle of death marches on.

Maurice begins his recollection of his participation in the third and final phase of Britain's evacuations...

Before we went to live in Kings Langley, to be closer to London, with my aunt, she took a rented house in a place which was closer to Watford called Tring. And to get to Tring by road, you used to have to go through Watford. And on the way from Watford to Tring it must have been about 20 miles. There was an airfield. And on that airfield was American planes. And you could see them loading up through the day with bombs.

Did you see those American planes airborne?

Yes. And they always used to be pretty low because they were landing or taking off from that airfield. They were not fighters.

U.S. Army Air Corps B-17 bomber takes-off from an English airfield

Heavy planes. And after the war you didn't see any planes there at all. Because you know, when you go away on a trip, on a drive, an afternoon drive, if you happened to go past there, I'd always look to see where the planes were. It was dilapidated. I got interested in airplanes, building models. And even when I was older and married I used to build. These were sailplanes—I forgot that.

Maurice with his "sailplane"

I always remember as well that the house which my aunt had in Tring was at the top of a hill. And at the bottom of the hill which must have been half a mile from the main road, there was a co-op shop and it had a glass roof. Glass panels on the roof. And one of the things that I liked doing was going on the road, level with their house, and down this slope and everything was this co-op shop. And I used to like throwing stones at the roof. And one day the manager caught me. He suddenly appeared and grabbed me by the collar and he was going to tell the police about me.

You were a bugger, weren't you?
Yeah. He came out of nowhere and was waiting on me.

* * *

Around this time Maurice's father was presented with the opportunity to begin a new business venture back in Hackney, opening a greengrocer shop. Being a tailor by trade, he found himself to be in great need of Sissy's expertise in setting-up and running the business (she had experience running a kosher butcher shop), but the 100-mile distance from Tring to London was far too great a daily commute for her. Before long, our perpetual evacuees were saying goodbye to Tring and setting up home base much closer to London—in the historic village of Kings Langley.

CHAPTER NINE

THE VILLAGE OF KINGS LANGLEY

In the county of Hertfordshire, situated some 20 miles to the northwest of London's center lays the historic village of Kings Langley. The village was once the location of a royal palace bearing its name—Kings Langley Palace. Its palatial gardens provided the setting for Act III, Scene IV of the Bard, Sir William Shakespeare's tragic play: *Richard II*. Edmund of Langley, the first Duke of York was entombed in the village's twelfth century parish Church of All Saints in 1402.[66] Another little known fact is that former U.S. President Jimmy Carter can trace his roots back to Kings Langley, where his ancestors bearing the Carter name resided between the years 1361-1588.[67] Of modern historical interest, the Polish underground army based secret headquarters

66 "Kings Langley - Our Heritage," Kings Langley Local History & Museum Society, Accessed November 21, 2016. http://www.kingslangley.org.uk/index.htm.
67 Humphrey, Robert, "The Carters of Kings Langley—The President's Roots," Hertfordshire Genealogy. Accessed November 21, 2016, http://www.hertfordshire-genealogy.co.uk/data/ books/books-1/ book0189-carter.html.

in the village during World War II—somewhat ironic given that the subject of our story is the son of a Polish refugee.[68]

Towards the end of the war, my mother spoke to my father and they had a friend who was in the greengrocery business:  vegetables, fruit. And they talked my father into owning a business in Hackney. And my father couldn't do it on his own, so my mother had to come back to London. And she brought me back to London at the same time. And the raids were still going on. And she wanted to get away where she could have easy access to London.

So these were buzz bombs that were coming down? The V-1's?

They were the V-2s. The rockets. V-1 was the bug, and V-2 was the rocket. And she found this school which is evacuating children to a place called Kings Langley, which is about 20 miles north of Watford. Watford is north of London. And he found this house that had an extra room in the back of the house, which was made up like a bedroom, where you could eat as well. So she rented this one room in the back of the house, and so we had two beds in it, and we stayed there. And occasionally she used to go back to London, and I was with friends in Kings Langley. And my aunt, I had an aunt, and she was married, and she wanted to

---

68 Peszke, Michael, Alfred, The Polish Underground Army, the Western Allies, and the Failure of Strategic Unity in World War II (London: McFarland and Company, Inc., Publishers, 2005), 53.

get out of London to avoid the bombs. She came down to Kings Langley, and she found a place and rented. So there was someone else in the village that was part of the family. And this aunt looked after me well.

When you were in Kings Langley, do you remember going to school?
There was a school, but it was downtown. We lived a couple of miles north of it. But it was downtown. But I missed the basic educational things that kids do. They take you by your age and they put you in a class, and you join in the best you can. She sent me to school, the local school, but I didn't get on well with the other children, because they kept on calling me a Londoner. And I must have been twelve. I must have been age about twelve and a half at that stage. She used to sometimes go to London and I had to stay there on my own—overnight. And I'll always remember I wanted to get back to London to my parents. And there was a public telephone box near where I lived in Kings Langley, and I used to call home from this telephone box. I was so afraid I would be taunted. I was taunted by the other children.

They used to make up stories about me. And this was a bad time, so what I'd done, I used to go to school at a certain time in the morning, say 8:30. I used to walk to school. So what I decided to do one week, leave home, or leave where I was at 8:30 in the morning, and instead of walking to school, I walked to the canal. The canal runs through Watford—Grand Union Canal. You've probably heard of it. And I used to walk around this canal, watch the boats, the tugs, go along and coming up to the locks, locks would open, water would go into the locks, to raise the tugs to the next level, and it would continue down the canal. And there were these tugs going in the opposite direction, and used to have the opposite effect. They would come up, close the locks doors, and then open slightly, open the locks, and the tugs would carry on. And I used to enjoy walking down the canal, and I used to be there all day playing hooky, and going home at the right time, like I used to go home from school.

I remember one day, when I was doin' this, it poured rain. And I caught a cold. So my aunt made me stay in bed one morning so I could get rid of my cold. Well, must have been about 10 o'clock in the morning, all quiet, because her husband used to commute to London to his business. So it was just her in the house and me. But I was in the bedroom. Around 10 o'clock on this Monday morning, there was a ring at the doorbell. Front door- bell. And all quiet. My aunt wondered who was at the door. And I was in bed upstairs, but I could hear the conversation. It was a school board man. And he said, "I'm inquiring, Maurice Levitt was not at school last week. What was the problem?" So my aunt says, "Pardon me, but he was at school." Well, it all came out that I played hooky that week, and caught a cold, and that was the situation. On Sunday my mother appeared, took me home. And that was it.

Took you home to London?
Yes.

So it worked.

* * *

Although four difficult months of war with Germany remained, the allied capture of the German V-2 launch sites in Peenemunde ended the Nazi threat to London and southwest England, and with that, the final stage of the Battle of Britain came to an end, allowing Maurice to return to his East Hackney home for good in January 1945.

CHAPTER TEN

FINAL THOUGHTS AND REFLECTIONS

"I remember the parade at the end of the war—celebrations, and at Buckingham Palace—Churchill, and all these different countries marching."

Maurice Levitt, 2005 - age seventy-two

The Cost of Evacuation

Well, what I was saying is, the other day I was thinking of the situation that I was in when I was evacuated at a young age, is how it affects your thoughts with respect to your mother and father. Because your mother and father as you grow up have a bigger effect on you than you think. And if you're moving from one home to another home to strangers, you seem to lose some of your thoughts for your own parents. There's something you miss.

Maurice at his aunt's back-garden tea party in happier, pre-war days

And I found that it's happened to me. Lots of things went on. That's how your life's been part off

I mean to say I always remember that one particular time, Lord Haw-Haw was speaking on the general radio, and my father rushed to radio and sat next to it with his ear to the loud speaker to listen to what he was saying every day—Lord Haw-Haw. He was issuing broadcasts internationally.

By Radio Berlin?

Yes, yes. But the thing is that being evacuated to different homes, you miss something as an individual. And I think it's affected me. I remember sometimes, I can visualize, looking at things even now, and remembering what things looked like, and shelters, and the people who were living in the shelters. I told you the time when the "all clear" sounded, and everyone was coming out of the shelter, and the guns went off. The army was emptying their barrels, their gun barrels, of loaded shells. The only way they could do that was to fire them off. And everyone rushing back to the shelter. And I remember at one stage, my father...because my father was always looking for work, because there was little tailoring work during the war. And he was out of a job. And there used to be a union. The tailors belonged to a union that helped get jobs. And how they used to do it, there was a headquarters in use at the end of London, and the tailors used to go there Sunday morning, standing on the pavement, talking to each other about potential jobs.

Just waiting to get work?

Well, yes, because with all of the bombing on, places and workshops were being shattered, you know? Always remember them meeting outside the union on a Sunday morning...worked for companies, small companies. They probably employed around five to ten people.

They required tailors.

But I think being evacuated on and off in different places certainly made a difference to me. But I often wondered how it affected me being sent away and having little contact with my family. Family, parents, aunts, uncles.

Because even though you were with Cissy, you still missed …

My father. Yes. There's a lot to take in. There were certain things that affected you. But hey, we survived.

Education

My best time at the preliminary schools was back in London. I did go to school before the war. Well, you know what happened when my mother took me the first day?

Maurice and Cissy in his college years

The first day I ever went to school, my mother took me and introduced me to the headmistress, and the headmistress took me to the classroom where all the children were, and that school had many floors. There was lots of stairs. And every afternoon you were put to bed. They had a classroom with beds. And every afternoon you used to go to that classroom and sleep—a nap. But the first day after my mother had delivered me to the school, my mother went away from home and when she got home, who was standing on the doorstep? I ran out of school when she left. Across the main road. Raced home. Back way. And waited for mother to come home. "What are you doing here? I left you at school? Come on, back you go." She took me back to school. I'll always remember that. I'll never forget it, never forget it. One thing I found was that seeing how I was moved from different locations and schools, my education wasn't like the education that we know of today because each particular school and what they were teaching, and then you go somewhere else, to another school.

Were you scared when you had to start in a new school, having been from the city?

Well, you know, you keep quiet and a lot of the other kids don't know you and some of them take the mick out of you and everything. Also, you notice we were having bacon. That I liked.

Did you tell them you weren't supposed to have bacon?
Yes.

What did they say?
"Up to you."

And I didn't really start a planned education until I was about 12.

Which would be after the war?

Right, it was. When I returned home. And it did affect me. But fortunately, I had a good teacher at the local school which I went to, and we got on well together – pupil and teacher. And he arranged when I was 14 that I go to technical college. And then my education expanded to anything you can think of. Physics, mathematics, geography, English, technical drawing, workshop, using lathes, using machines, carpentry. It was a good technical college. I enjoyed going to the technical college. I enjoyed the subjects. And always remember with the technical school, if we'd done something wrong, they used to give you a strap. And I'll always remember, I had it once. I'd done something wrong. And

The athlete Maurice with his father at a track and field event

you have to go to this table, bend down on the table, with your "tuchas"* hanging out, and the headmaster would come with a strap and give you a terrific bang on the backside. No, that was the best time, at technical college. Because I enjoyed doing the work. I enjoyed it. Using lathes, drilling machines, mini-machines. And then when I left school, the teacher got me to sign up to be an apprentice with GEC. General Electric. And I was nearly 17 then.

And GE took me on as an apprentice at 17, for three years, to be in the design office. And they also gave me one day off a week to go to school, college. And when I finished the apprenticeship at age 21, I was then valid to be called up in the draft. But considering

I went to school one day a week, I continued my education and they didn't take me in the draft until 25.

Serving in the Royal Air Force

And then I was called up and I was in the Air Force. And as soon as I joined, I was promoted, because I had an education. And had three propellers on my shoulder.

Senior Aircraftman Levitt

What were you, a sergeant?

No, senior aircraftman. I went in at 25 and I came out at 27. So I served about two years. And when I went in, you do your screen ration and when I finished the screen ration, I then posted. And you could be posted anywhere around the world. And at that time the war had just started on the Suez. And I was fine about being sent to the Suez. Because I think the Air Force had air stations there. And I was sent to Chippenham. That's the West Country of England, to be educated again, for radar—working the radar equipment. So I went there, and I think it was a nine-month course and you had tests every month. And you were allowed the weekend off—catch a coach to take me back to London, because I was home every weekend. And the camp occupied a large area, and the main road went past the camp and on the other side of the main road there was the hills, and on this hill there was a

Maurice with his RAF mates

cow. No, it wasn't a cow. It was a horse, which had been sculptured in the ground on the mountain. And every Wednesday afternoon was sports afternoon. One sports afternoon, a lot of the guys went across the road to the statue of this horse and put a cock on it. And all hell blew over in the camp. It was probably about 20 feet long, this horse, and they all were carving away, and digging out because it was black sandstone. It wasn't earth. It was sandstone. It was white against the green grass. I'll never forget that.

His Cousin Evelyn

So after you started evacuating with your mom, what happened to Evelyn?

After Somerset, when her father took me home, Evelyn stayed on for a period. And then when she came back to London

First cousins with their "mums"

she was older. She was a clever girl. And her mother did not get on well with her father. And the father got ill and passed away after the war. The mother used to go to the underground shelters. You know the tube trains? People used to go down there for shelter. And she met a gentleman there. And when Evelyn's father died, she then got with this other man. And after the war, they got married. And in 1948, they decided to move to Australia. And they took Evelyn with. And Evelyn went to college and she was passed out as a dental surgeon.

Another dental surgeon in the family?

Mm-hm. Yes, she would be a dental surgeon. He had a business in knitwear. And she done all right for herself. And Evelyn herself, when she got married, she got married to a fairly wealthy husband. It's a big family on my mother's side. On my father's side, it wasn't a big family. And he was out of work for a long time, before the war. There were little jobs. And that's why their friend talked them into owning a green grocery business.

Did they make a go of it? Did it do well?

Comfortable.

His Father Abram

The Records Department[69] testified that the following record exists in the records of birth in 1897: It took place in the town of Mshonuv at 10 a.m. 46-year-old Moshek Juda Kisi-

---

69 Abram's birth was recorded under the authority the burgomaster of Mshonuv in Poland.

levich, as his published name, who resides in town, appeared in person and in the presence of a witness, thirty-six-year-old church attendant Abram Hil Winetrob, and declared that the infant was born by his forty-four-year-old legitimate wife Hanna Gitli, in this town. The name Abram was given to the infant...that's my father...during the religious ceremony of clipping.

Do you know what clipping is?

Circumcision?

This record was read to the declarer and witnesses, inside of it said he was illiterate. Polish stamps. And this document is now his birth certificate. Dated 1921.

So his name was Abraham.

No. Abram. When they called me up for an Aliyah, in Synagogue, when they called me up to read from the Torah in the Synagogue, they give you your name and your father's name. They call me by Moshe ben Avraham. Maurice, son of Avraham. And I would go up to the Torah and read the Torah. That's the Jewish way. I'm the only one that gets called up now. The Rabbi remarked about it two weeks ago. Every Saturday I'm getting called up to the second Aliyah to say prayers and when the Aliyah's finished I finish the prayer in the book.

That's an honor.

As the Rabbi said, I'm a consistent to be called up.

My father...there were a lot of pogroms going on in Poland. It's the Polish people were attacking the Jews. And they were going to the villages and killing loads of Jews. And what happened to the Jews, if they could manage it, they would try and get out of Poland into France, and then go to England, and then go to America. But they had to have had the money. And they would have to stay in certain areas or countries awhile to earn money for the next trip they were taking.

So basically refugees?

Right. And my father, he was in the Polish Army. And he was wounded, he got shot in the leg.

By the Russians—because the Russians were fighting the Poles. And the big laugh...the Russian Army at that stage...there was a big area which was women soldiers. And one of the women soldiers shot my father in the leg. And that was a big laugh. And after the war was finished, which I don't know when, but it was before 1922, my father decided it's time to go to America, as other people or other members of his family had done.

I didn't know your father had family members that went before him.

No brothers and sisters, but nephews and cousins and that. And he traveled across Europe. And once he told me he was traveling to a certain part of Germany on the train, he had no ticket, and when the inspector came 'round for tickets, he hid underneath the seats. And he finally made it to Paris, and he lived in Paris for a couple of years. Then he didn't have the money to go to America from Paris. He traveled then to the French coast and then, in a boat, they were taken to England. So as I know it, he went by train from Poland to Paris. But on the route, he didn't have any ticket for the train. Now thinking of your geography, he got to Paris, and he started working. He started working to get some money so he could go to Belgium. And once he was in Belgium, he then started working there again to try and get to England. And he couldn't get enough money so he got friendly with a sailor whose boat was in port one day and explained his situation to him, and this sailor said, "I'll get you across to England." And that's what happened.

* * *

On more than one occasion, Maurice told me that the Jews from continental Europe, who did not have the money to get all the way to America, ended up settling in England—as did his father. That is not to say that they were welcomed with open arms by the British government—a fact that the thousands of German Jews who were fleeing pre-war Nazi Germany in the early 1930s could have testified to. For example: during the early years of Hitler's regime, a time when England and the rest of the western world was already wallowing in the Great Depression, Britain's Minister of Labor was confronted with the prospect of taking in thousands of German-Jewish refugees. His response was quite telling in terms of his government's view of this immigration crisis. The Minister essentially expressed that he was "not prepared" to take the responsibility to agree to take any measures which might result in an increase in Britain's already high unemployment figures. The Jews simply were not wanted by King George's government, which saw no prospects of taking them into any of its colonies either—least of all Palestine where anti-Jewish sentiment was prevalent. Eventually, the British government, having accepted a financial "guarantee" from the Jewish community, acquiesced and began accepting Jewish refugees from Germany with the condition that they register with the police upon entry.[70]

British war-time policy and reaction in regards to Nazi Germany' atrocities against Europe's Jews was not much better. Initially, with the outbreak of war in September 1939 the British government reacted swiftly in response to reports of these crimes against humanity that were transmitted to Britain by the Polish underground and certain American journalists. As early as October, the government issued a white paper on German atrocities. Curiously, the report only addressed those committed in the pre-war years. Although the pamphlet that emerged from the paper sold well, it was later judged to have been a propaganda failure. Thereafter, the government resolved to avoid atrocity propaganda as a matter of course as evidenced by the Ministry of Information planning committee's decision of July of 1941.

The committee concluded that it should use only a "limited amount of horror" in home propaganda while referencing only "indisputably innocent people" excluding cases involving "violent political opponents"—and the Jews.[71]

The interview continues…

When did your father lose contact with his family?

He lost contact with his family in 1939. At least that's when Germany started with Poland. And I can't remember my father ever calling Poland.

---

70 Deborah Dwork and Robert Jan Van Pelt, Flight from the Reich: Refugee Jews 1933-1946 (New York: W. W. Norton & Company, 2009), 25.
71 Walter Laqueur, The Holocaust Encyclopedia (New Haven and London: Yale University Press, 2001), 90.

Did he try to reach them by writing letters?

The only time he tried writing letters was after the war, and then sending the letters to the Red Cross for their help. But the only thing that came out of it was his nephew, and I think I told you about him. The one who wanted to go to Russia in the beginning and went to Germany instead. And I've tried to contact him in recent years in Canada. No reply. He's probably dead now. But there is part of that family that settled in New York. And I also said to Naomi the other day, "I'll bet you there's some part of my family living in New York on my father's side." Because what happened was my father left Poland in 1922 to follow other members of his family who had gone to America. Yes. This was in 1922. And my father wanted to join him because he wasn't doing anything in Poland. They had the pogroms and he wanted to get out of all that.

Oh, yes, he had family, older family. And he then stayed with his…I don't know whether…it must have been an uncle or an aunt. Because I remember those two, the husband and the wife. I met them. And he stayed with them. I always remember them because the husband, I didn't like. Because if you sat on a chair, and you tilted it, he said that would ruin the chair. And he had a big walking stick, and he would bang the walking stick on the chair to make it sit up straight. I'll always remember that. I'll never forget it, never forget it. And they lived near a big brewery on the East end of London.

And so that's how my father came to England. Once he got to England he started looking for work, but he never got enough money to get to America. So that's how he met my mother.

What did your father do on an average day during the war?

Well, a lot depends on if he was working. Because in England or in London, in wartime, high unemployment because lots of houses and workshops were being bombed. And people were out of work. And the tailoring trade had a union. And most of the tailors belonged to the union. And due to the unemployment, on a Sunday morning, the union would open its door in East London and the tailors would go there and I can remember this as if I'm looking at it now. The tailors would all be standing on the pavement outside waiting for someone to come up and ask them if they wanted a job. And therefore the out-of-work tailors will all come to this union in the hope of getting a job the following week.

When my father was working, I remember him once going to work in the morning. And he saw what happened in a certain district that the bus was going, where a bomb had hit a bus and a bus was in a big hole in the road. There was such a drastic explosion, that's what happened. It used to go on.

And he was in the Home Guard, too?

Yes. They never went to the community shelters. They wanted something to do to help. They would join the Home Guard. And I always remember, I can visually see it now. The Home Guard seniors taking the ones who were just joining to show them how to work a stirrup pump. You know what that is? That's a pump, a manual pump for water. One end of the pipe would go in the water, and you would pump and it would come out the other end of the pipe. And if an incendiary bomb used to land, that's how they used to try and put an incendiary bomb out with a stirrup pump.

I remember they used to do the instruction in London Fields. It was a big park near where we lived. And I remember my father when they were showing him to do it, if you started here, and let's say the bomb was over there, and they told you you've got to get there

Home Guardsmen deploying a stirrup pump

quickly before the explosion before the incendiary bomb explodes. And I remember him running towards the bomb, the fake bomb, with the end of the pipe, with the stirrup, and somebody else was going to pump, and they were running towards where the bomb was and he slipped, and he slid towards the bomb. I can remember that.

So they would pour water on the incendiary bomb before it went off?
Yes.

Wasn't that dangerous? It could have gone off at any moment, right?
Well, an incendiary bomb is not an explosive bomb. It's for fire. Phosphorous.
But as I say, he was many times going down Sunday morning to the union to try and get a job.

Did he have buddies?
A few. People didn't know if they'd see you the next day, with the bombing. But he used to go through a lot. And things were

a lot simpler in those times. I must say, even in the house, the toilets, were outside toilets. Bathrooms? No bathrooms in houses. You'd see those communal bath-houses in London. And after the war, my parents installed a bathroom and an internal toilet. All the things that come to my mind.

Did you hear anything about what the Nazis were doing to the Jews in Europe?
    It was rumored.

What kinds of things were they saying to you?
    Well, it was only reported once the camps were liberated. Sometimes we used to find pilots who had survived their crashed planes and they were picked up by the locals, not the Germans. This is in France or Belgium or Holland. And they used to tell them what was going on in the camps with the Jews.

Really? The German pilots you're talking about?
    No, the Allied pilots.

How would they know?
    Well, they knew.

The Fate of His Family

After the war, my father tried to contact his family and there was no one there. And the Red Cross helped people to try and locate what happened to their family. I helped him try and locate some of the family. This is all letters that were written.

So he contacted the Red Cross...how long did it take for them to get back to him?

Couple of weeks. What happened was that he contacted the Red Cross and they had agents in Europe, and they would go to different cities to try and find out...because the Germans were good at record-keeping, and to try and find his family. But what brought him a lot of information was one of his nephews—before the war went to Russia. And before the war started, and then would come back to the family...and got all the family together and said that there was an impending war with Germany, and they should go with him back to Russia, where they'd be safe from the Germans. What turned out, the family said no. They're not going to relocate to Russia. They're staying where they are. The nephew said, well, he's going to move. And what he'd done, he never went back to Russia, but he went to Germany and got friendly with a German girl. And she hid him throughout the war. And they got married. And after the war, they went, or they were sent, to Canada. And he had to go back to Poland for something or other. I don't know whether it was to get recompense for what Germany had done to their family. And on his way, he stopped in London and contacted my father.

What year would that have been?

Oh, that was probably about '47 or '48. So my father met him for the first time.

Did you meet him?

Yes. And he stayed I think two days in London and went off to Germany, and we never heard from him since. I tried finding him. He's a doctor—turned out to be a doctor. And I tried to find him a few times. But first of all, he was a lot older than me, so he's probably dead. Who knows? Looking for him, but no.

So my father never went back to Poland. What was there to see? There was nothing there to see. What the Red Cross did find out was that a couple of the family went to certain camps where they were put...you know, killed. And I've got the information there on … I thought I had it.

Maurice spent a few minutes unsuccessfully leafing through his file folders for the precious letter his grandmother had written to his father from soon to be German-occupied Poland. Sadly, as of the conclusion of this project, the letter remained missing.

***

When your father found out that the entire family was killed in the camps, did he find out all at once?

Piece by piece.

Maurice solemnly reveals the tragic truth in his memoirs:

"So finally the world was at peace, and all the horrors then began to come out of the German occupation of Europe and how the Jews suffered. This was a bad time for my father, as all his brothers and sisters were in Poland in the Holocaust and died in the Nazi concentration camps in Poland. He tried tracing them after the war but without success. I did not know any of my father's brothers, sisters or my grandparents on my father's side. I only knew some of my father's cousins who had moved to London before my father came to England in 1922."[72]

---

72 Levitt, "Memories of Maurice Levitt", 16.

***

On September 29, 1939, Hitler effectively foretold the fate of Maurice's family, as he revealed his opinion of the newly conquered people in Poland with his old party crony Alfred Rosenberg: "The Poles—a thin Germanic layer underneath frightful material. The Jews (the Nazi warlord continued) were the most appalling people one could imagine."[73] Of all the Jewish people living in Nazi-controlled Europe it was unquestionably the Jews of Poland—a nation with a large Jewish population, and long and shameful history of antisemitism characterized by its notorious "Pogroms"—who received the brunt of Hitler's so-called "Final solution to the Jewish question." In fact, on the eve of the German invasion, the majority of the Polish population supported their nation's move to deprive its 3.5 million Jews of their rights to live in Poland. Indeed, after the German invasion, the Polish government in exile's attitude appeared to be equally ambivalent toward Poland's Jews.

When all was said and done, there were only 310,000 Polish Holocaust survivors out of the over 3.5 million Jews living in Poland when war broke out in September 1939. It has been estimated that only 15,000 of the 3.2 million were saved by the Poles or less than one half of one percent.[74]

We continued...

It must have been awfully hard for him.

It was because I remember him listening to the radio many times in the war, of the German Lord Haw-Haw. He used to make

---

73 Saul Friedlander, The Years of Extermination: Nazi Germany and the Jews 1939-1945 (New York: Harper Collins Publishers, 2007), 11.

74 Jack R. Fischel, The A to Z of the Holocaust (Oxford: The Scarecrow Press, 2005), 186.

The only remaining evidence of Maurice's family members who remained in Poland are old photographs such as this one taken sometime in the mid-1920s. From left to right: Abram's sister Leah and her husband, two of his cousins, and his brother Chaim—all of whom tragically perished in the Holocaust. Bottom center: Abram's mother Hanna—who died before the war in 1925.

a report which my father used to listen to on the radio. It was a popular program in London. And my father used to listen to it.

But no, he didn't see any family anymore. I've got one letter to my father from his mother.

Yes, so all these things made a turbulent life for me.

They did, they did. But you survived it, and you raised a good family, and here we are. Boy. And your dad? He ended up in Arizona?

Yes.

And your mother.

Yes. My father sat on a rocking chair and died. Yes.

And my wife was right there with him. She saw the whole thing.

Yes. I always remember he was always constipated. And that morning he was *really* constipated, and he wouldn't get off the toilet. And I was trying to help him, you know? And he got off the toilet, and went and sat in the lounge on his rocking chair, next thing he was asleep.

Passing it Down

This has been great. I think I've got a lot of wonderful, precious parts of your life, and this story is important.

Well, I've had a lot of experiences and some good, some bad.

Well, thank God you got out of London and lived to tell the story.

And missed being killed that night with the mine. That was the closest that I've been.

Thank you, Dad, thanks for doing this with me.

No, it's interesting. I think a lot of people should speak to their youngsters when they get older to tell them about their bringing up and their life. Because there's always ... you speak to me one day and say, "I wish I had asked my parents this, I wish I had asked them that." Because I think everyone should leave a history of their own life. For their children who always want to know about it.

I should do that someday too because you never know...I'm 58.

I'm 84.

EPILOGUE

Just over three years have come and gone since Maurice and I conducted the interviews. He will be 87 years of age at the end of this month and continues to live in the same ranch-style house in South Bend with his beloved wife Naomi, who has assumed the role of his loving caregiver. Sadly, the foggy banks of dementia have rolled-in—clouding Maurice's once vivid memory. As if that were not enough, he has also been diagnosed with the onset of Parkinson's disease. Despite these health challenges which have both mentally and physically slowed him down (Maurice now relies upon a cane–and on his worst days–a walker) he remains, for the most part, lucid and cognitively coherent. He also continues to show a keen interest in his book, rarely failing to ask, "How is the book coming along, Charles?" Encouragingly, a recent neurological exam left the doctor quite astonished at Maurice's firm handshake leading him to conclude that there was no Parkinson's related progression since his last visit. Further, Maurice continues to log 30 minutes per day on his stationary bike as has been his practice for years. He continues to persevere with dogged resolve—after all, he *is* a son of East-Hackney.

Late last July our family decided to brave the thirty-mile, partially back-roads drive to the east shore of Lake Michigan for a

family cook-out with hopes of partaking in one of those spectacular mid-summer sunsets over the great lake. Laura, Elise and I picked-up Maurice and Naomi, while Katelyn and her husband Gage arranged to meet us at our favorite spot known as Weko Beach.

This was an increasingly rare yet joyous occasion that found us *all* together. Left to right is: our youngest daughter Elise, yours truly, our son-in-law Gage, our eldest daughter Katelyn, Naomi and Maurice. (Conspicuously absent is my lovely wife Laura who took the photo)

Having gorged ourselves on fresh salmon grilled to perfection along with homemade potato salad and coleslaw we collectively abandoned our picnic table and settled into beach chairs in anticipation of the solar spectacle. My toes barely had the chance to gain purchase into the warm sand when Laura announced, "Charles, Dad needs to use the lavatory. Could you take him?" Well, this was a first for both of us but it did not seem to bother Maurice whatsoever. I helped him out of his chair and he took me by the hand with that strong grip of his (also a first) as we began the 100 meters or so walk across the deep sand to the Weko Beach bathhouse.

We made it without incident entering the building through its beach-level lower entrance. Maurice utilized their facilities while I waited patiently.

We had barely begun our walk back to our family's picnic area when something wonderful happened between us. Just a few feet onto the beach we found ourselves facing the western horizon. As one, we stopped walking to marvel at the sun which had begun its descent over Lake Michigan. Overcome by the moment Maurice took my hand he was still holding into both of his and began to pray—for me! "Please God...may health, happiness and prosperity be upon your family." He then looked up into my eyes and urged me to join in by repeating the words "Please God". I solemnly did so with more than a little difficulty as I choked back my tears.

Maurice then repeated the beautiful prayer once more. When he finished his prayer I gave my "second father's" fragile old body a warm hug as the mid-summer sun slowly set on the watery horizon.

Gathering myself, and still somewhat overwhelmed with emotion, I resumed my mission to return Maurice to the bosom of his family. Finally, as we labored through the deep sand our conversation took-on a less serious tone:

"Dad, I'm almost finished with your book."
"Did you include my 'handsome' photograph?"

"Do you mean the one that makes you look like Errol Flynn?"
Looking down, I was delighted to see that once again that sparkle had returned to his eyes.
"Yes, that's the one!"

"You'll find it on page 36."

BIBLIOGRAPHY

Ambrosius Lloyd E. *Writing Biography: Historians and Their Craft.*
Lincoln: University of Nebraska Press. 2004.

Arnold-Forster, Mark. *The World at War.* New York: Stein and Day
Publishers, 1973.

Baker, James, Topographer. *A brief narrative of the French invasion, near
Fishguard Bay:*

Langley Local History & Museum Society Accessed November 21, 2016.
http://www.kingslangley.org.uk/index.html

Laqueur, Walter. *The Holocaust Encyclopedia.* New Haven and London:
Yale University Press, 2001.

Levitt, Maurice. "Memories of Maurice Levitt." Personal memoirs, South
Bend, Indiana, 2005.

Lewis, Martin. *Newport, Pem and Fishguard.* Summit:NPI Media Group,
1996.

Longmate, Norman. *Hitler's Rockets: the Story of the V-2s.* London:
Hutchinson and

Company Publishers Ltd., 1985.

Longmate, Norman. *How We Lived Then: a History of Everyday Life*

During the Second World War. London: Hutchinson and Company Publishers Ltd., 1971.

Longmate, Norman. *The GIs: The Americans in Britain 1942-1945.* New York: Charles Scribner's Sons, 1975.

Mackenzie, S.P. *The Home Guard.* New York: Oxford University Press, 1995.

Neil, Murray. "The Washingtons of Tring," *Tring & District Local History & Museum Society. 2013.*http://www.hertfordshigenealogy.co.uk/data/books/books-6/book-0632-washingtons-of-tring.htm.

Ogley, Bob. *Doodlebugs and Rockets: The Battle of the Flying Bombs.* Kent: Froglets Publications, 1995.

Overy, R.J. *The Air War.* New York: Stein and Day, 1981.

Parker, Keith A. "British evacuees in America during World War II." *Journal of American Culture* 17, no.4 (Winter 94 1994): 33.

Perris, G. H. (George Herbert), and G.H Perris. *Industrial History of Modern England.* [S.l.]: Kegan Paul Trench Trubner And Company Limited. http://tt5xg8qf8p.search.se-rialssolutions.com/?V=1.0&L=TT5XG8QF8P&S=JCs&C=TC_005409634&T=- marc.

Peszke, Michael, Alfred. *The Polish Underground Army, the Western Allies, and the Fail- ure of Strategic Unity in World War II.* London: McFarland and Company, Inc., Publishers, 2005.

Prall, Stuart E and Wilson, David H. *A History of England Volume I: Prehistory to 1714.*

Fort Worth: Holt, Rinehart and Winston, Inc., 1991.

Prall, Stuart E and Wilson, David H. *A History of England Volume II: 1603 to the Present.*

Fort Worth: Holt, Rinehart and Winston, Inc., 1991.

Ruggero, Ed. *The First Men In: U.S. Paratroops and the Fight to Save D-Day.* New York: HarperCollins Publishers, 2006.

Sereny, Gitta. *Into the Darkness: An Examination of Conscience.* New York: Vintage Books, 1983.

Shirer, William. *The Rise and Fall of the Third Reich.* New York: Simon and Schuster, 1960. *Styles and Methods of Writing Biographies, Oral Histories and Creative Non-fiction: Four Paradigm Transformations in Oral History,* Alistair Thomson the Oral History Review Vol. 34, No. 1 (Winter - Spring, 2007), pp. 49-70.

Summers, Julie. *When the Children Came Home: Stories of Wartime Evacuees.* New York: Simon and Schuster, 2011.

Tetzlaff, Monica. *Cultivating a New South: Abbie Holmes Christensen and the Politics of Race and Gender, 1832-1938.* Columbia: University of South Carolina Press, 2002.

Turkel, Studs. *The Good War: An Oral History of World War II.* New York: The New Press.

1984.

Welshman, John. *Churchill's Children.* New York: Oxford University Press, Inc., 2010.

Wikipedia contributors. "Battle of Britain." *Wikipedia, the Free Encyclopedia.* San Francisco:

Wikipedia Foundation, 17 Jul. 2016.

Wikipedia contributors. "Cerebos." *Wikipedia, the Free Encyclopedia.* San Francisco: Wikipedia Foundation, 12 Jan. 2016. Web. 22 Jul. 2016. Publications,1992.

Wikipedia contributors. "Fishguard." *Wikipedia, the Free Encyclopedia*. San Francisco: Wikipedia Foundation, 27 Jun. 2016.

Wikipedia contributors. "Kings Langley." *Wikipedia, the Free Encyclopedia*. San Francis- co: Wikipedia Foundation, 2 Jul. 2016.

Wikipedia contributors. "London Borough of Hackney." *Wikipedia, the Free Encyclopedia*. San Francisco: Wikipedia Foundation, 26 May. 2016.

Wikipedia contributors. "Somerset." *Wikipedia, the Free Encyclopedia*. San Francisco: Wikipedia Foundation, 10 Jul. 2016.

Wikipedia contributors. "Tring." *Wikipedia, the Free Encyclopedia*. San Francisco: Wiki- Encyclopedia Foundation, 16 Jul. 2016.

Wikipedia contributors."Northampton." *Wikipedia, the Free Encyclopedia*. San Francisco: Wikipedia Foundation, 18 Jul. 2016.

Wilson, Alan. *Hackney Memories*. Oxford: ISIS Publishing Ltd., 2004.

Woolf, S.J., *European Fascism*. New York: Random House Inc, 1968.

ABOUT THE AUTHOR

Charles C. Minx, Jr. was born to Charles C. Minx, Sr. and Dorothy M. Minx in South Bend Indiana in 1958. He was the youngest of their children having two older sisters Janice and Mary. From a very early age, Charles displayed a keen interest in history. His insatiable desire to learn led him to eventually enroll in a state college in Muncie, Indiana, where he earned a Bachelor of Arts in History from Ball State University in 1982. Along the way, Charles received the coveted "Childress Scholarship" for excellence in History.

After graduation, the call of the west found Charles in Santa Barbara, California. After establishing residency, he attended graduate school at the University of California, Santa Barbara's Public History program. This research-based program did not satisfy his "inner-teacher" so he withdrew mid-way through the first semester. After a couple of "fun" years in the Golden State, he moved to Connecticut where his family had relocated from their Indiana home. While in Connecticut, he earned his teaching certification in Social Sciences from Southern Connecticut State University in 1988.

Shortly after returning to Santa Barbara California in 1990, he met his future wife, Laura. In 1993, at the advanced age of 35 (and somewhat on a whim), Charles enlisted in the U.S. Army. He served six years in the reserve component under Special Operations Command. In 1994, Charles decided to take the technical path by returning to school and earning an Associate in Applied Science in Electrical Engineering Technology. This latest degree landed him a position in Silicon Valley. He and his wife Laura immediately purchased a home in the San Joaquin Valley and began raising their two girls, Katelyn and Elise. The disaster of 9/11 and its economic repercussions ended the so-called "Golden Age of Telecom" resulting in the closure of Charles's telecom test lab in 2002. This led to the end of California living for the Minx family.

Coming full circle, Charles returned to South Bend in early 2003, where he and his family began their lives anew. After a career in the aerospace industry, He had the opportunity to return to graduate school and earn his Master's degree. He did so in 2015, enrolling in the Master of Liberal Studies program at Indiana University South Bend. There, he received the program's "Excellence in MLS" award for the 2016-17 academic year. Most importantly, it was Charles's graduate thesis project—an oral history of his own father-in-law—that both laid the foundation for, and served as the impetus of, this very important primary source historical account.